Praise for *Leadership Dialogu*

Our leadership teams have never needed more training in their roles as they do now during these challenging times. And as the original *Leadership Dialogues* has proven to be such a powerful tool for leaders, I believe *Leadership Dialogues II* will be another important step in the process of developing and improving their skills.

Harris and West-Burnham offer a serious reflection on leadership with very interesting resources which enable the reflourishing of previous thinking on the topic, and they expertly tackle a wide variety of key points – from the importance of useful meetings to the real purpose of education – from the most particular points up to the most general and crucial ones.

Juan Carlos García, Pedagogical, Pastoral and Innovation Department, Escuelas Católicas de Madrid

At a time when school leadership is pressurised into consisting of leading a school to a decent set of exam results and an inspection that keeps 'them' off your back for a few more years, *Leadership Dialogues II* puts the heart, the soul, the integrity and the moral purpose back into its core. It combines common sense, wisdom and research based practice to great effect in imbuing school leaders with the tools, knowledge and bravery to be the leaders that any education system truly deserves.

Ian Gilbert, founder, Independent Thinking

In the same way that the original *Leadership Dialogues* became an indispensable manual for reviewing the fundamental aspects of school leadership, *Leadership Dialogues II* takes leadership teams on similar journeys into deeper and currently relevant areas for review; from securing equity and engagement to analysing the use of research in education, via a debate on the purpose of education. Such is the quality and depth of content and the ease of reading, leadership development is unavoidable.

Don't expect that this book will give you all the answers, however – it won't. What it will do is stimulate and structure thinking, and challenge leadership teams to *find* the answers from within their own schools. This book is the catalyst, not the solution.

Paul Bannister, Junior School Head Teacher, Jerudong International School

From cover to cover *Leadership Dialogues II* provides a rich array of highly engaging themes as well as practical tools; yet it serves no straight answers. It is a gem of a read, a book many school leaders have always hoped someone would write just for them in order to boost their leadership capacity, help explore sensitive topics through asking relevant questions, back them up when empowering staff and stakeholders to generate optimum solutions for students, schools and communities, and provide a shot of inspiration to build a society centred around improved well-being.

Janja Zupančič, Head Teacher, Louis Adamic Grosuplje Primary School, Slovenia

To address today's issues, and those beyond the horizon, we need support in finding solutions, and these are best constructed through well-formed dialogue – which begins by interrogating good practice before moving on to building consensus. This is the distinct aim of Dave Harris and John West-Burnham's *Leadership Dialogues II*.

So whether you are looking at challenges as diverse as developing middle leadership, considering alternative staffing models or raising the achievement of disadvantaged pupils, this book will provide evidence and research to consider, questions to help form discussions and, finally, guidance to help you act to make your school or trust as effective as possible.

Paul K. Ainsworth, academy adviser for a system leader multi-academy trust and author of *Middle Leadership* and *Get That Teaching Job!*

Leadership Dialogues II has the moral imperative of education at its heart: to create happy, confident and successful learners. School leaders reading this book will be encouraged to focus on the key questions they have about their own settings and to then take action based on a holistic view of learning and learners, collective responsibility and shared mental models. Educational wisdom, insightful dialogue and challenge are balanced with simple yet extremely powerful reflective tools. *Leadership Dialogues II* is a flexible resource that will galvanise leadership of positive change in schools based upon the learning needs of children and young people.

Jan Gimbert, education adviser and trainer

Leadership Dialogues was always my 'go to' book when planning for more strategic work towards school improvement. This follow-up picks up from where the first left off, adding sections on topics such as purpose, engagement and developing evidence based practice.

Some of the chapters are perennial favourites when it comes to educational thinking; however, the difference with this is the fresh perspectives and divergent thinking it provides. I particularly like the theme of doing things differently – which other educational book would give you the idea of looking at your school as if it were a car, as Harris and West-Burnham have?

Essential reading for those of us lucky enough to be leading education.

Keith Winstanley, Head Teacher, Castle Rushen High School

Relevant, practical and packed full of great resources, *Leadership Dialogues II* is essential reading for leaders at all levels in schools. It offers both theory and practice, which is great for busy leaders, and provides a really good platform for reflection, thinking and dialogue. The authors really understand the complexities of leadership, and inspire possible solutions and ways forward in a thoughtful but practical way. I highly recommend this book.

Stephen Logan, Deputy Head Teacher, Malet Lambert School

Asking some of the biggest questions of our time, the hugely influential and respected Dave Harris and John West-Burnham provide an external perspective and a range of support materials to aid schools' internal constructive dialogues and decision making. Their think pieces and diagnostic review tools aim to help school leaders make value led, deep rooted, wise decisions for the pupils and staff they lead.

Far ranging and simply brilliant, *Leadership Dialogues II* is a 'group reader' that all those working in schools should use and engage with.

Stephen Tierney, CEO, Blessed Edward Bamber Catholic Multi Academy Trust, blogger (leadinglearner.me) and author of *Liminal Leadership*

LEADERSHIP
DIALOGUES II

LEADERSHIP
DIALOGUES II

LEADERSHIP IN TIMES OF CHANGE

DAVE HARRIS AND
JOHN WEST-BURNHAM

Crown House Publishing Limited
www.crownhouse.co.uk

First published by
Crown House Publishing
Crown Buildings, Bancyfelin, Carmarthen, Wales, SA33 5ND, UK
www.crownhouse.co.uk
and
Crown House Publishing Company LLC
PO Box 2223, Williston, VT 05495, USA
www.crownhousepublishing.com

British Library of Cataloguing-in-Publication Data
A catalogue entry for this book is available from the British Library.

Print ISBN 978-178583256-7
Mobi ISBN 978-178583322-9
ePub ISBN 978-178583323-6
ePDF ISBN 978-178583324-3

LCCN 2014958604

Printed and bound in the UK by
TJ International, Padstow, Cornwall

Acknowledgements

We are very grateful to the many individuals who have contacted us to tell us how useful they found the original *Leadership Dialogues*. We know of schools who use it as a regular part of the leadership meetings and others who have developed teacher leadership training programmes around it. This was always our aim – not to provide answers, but to promote dialogue.

In a time when many still judge education using simplistic, data-driven, archaic techniques, it is heartening to meet so many people whose only focus is to help young people become happy, confident and successful learners.

To those brave, passionate and dedicated leaders – thank you.

Keep making a difference!

Contents

How to use the book

This is not a book containing all the answers. It is a book containing many of the questions that will help you work with your colleagues to find the answers for your own school for the community in which you work.

We are living in times in which people are looking for both simple answers and detailed instructions to help them progress to their goals. But in a period of rapid change, like the one we are in now (at least for the foreseeable future), there is no step-by-step guide, there is no instruction manual – only strong tools to support you on your journey.

There will be similar themes underlying the problems faced by schools across the world, but the precise issues tend to be very specific to each school. The best people to interrogate the problems and find the answers are those of you working in, leading and governing these schools every day.

We have produced a book that we believe you will find helpful as a means of promoting constructive dialogue and debate, which will result in the generation of feasible solutions for your school.

For each of the eight themes in this book we have assembled five sections, each of which contains an outline on why this is an important topic, some key quotes to engage your thinking, a 10 minute discussion to provoke debate, some questions for your team to consider and, to help frame the dialogue's outcomes, downloadable resources for each section. The resources are often in tabular form and relate to the material, which means you can use them with little extra preparation. The only thing you have to do is:

To think

and then *discuss*

and then *act*.

The eight themes explored in this book are:

1 Securing equity and engagement
2 Clarifying the purpose of education
3 Middle leadership – the engine room of the school
4 Managing resources
5 Learning and technology
6 Education beyond the school
7 Alternative staffing models
8 Developing evidence based practice

These complement those explored in the first *Leadership Dialogues* book:

A Effective leadership
B Thinking strategically
C Leading innovation and change
D Leading teaching and learning
E Leading and managing resources
F Leading people
G Collaboration
H Engaging with students, parents and community

Schools/groups of schools have found that book to be a useful backbone for their own staff development courses to support both established and developing leaders. In some cases, materials have been co-designed with the authors and then most of the sessions delivered by staff from within the schools. The key point is to make sure that the materials chosen are relevant to the situations being faced by the learners and suited to the situation of the school.

We believe the answers for school improvement usually lie within many of the people already in the institution. Leadership is about causing those changes to happen. Our book is intended to add an outside perspective, a list of ideas to consider and questions to ask. Not to make schools develop in the way *we* think, but to help schools develop in the best way for the future of *their* pupils.

Do not hesitate to contact either of the authors to discuss ways to adapt the materials in both books to suit your own specific demands.

Introduction

Leadership learning through dialogue

If learning and leadership are both seen as primarily social processes, then dialogue is the medium and the message. Leaders work through various permutations of social interaction in order to engage as leaders. They can be highly effective and make a significant impact to the extent that they have the skills and behaviours appropriate to dialogue.

High quality dialogue is fundamental to almost every aspect of leadership; not only does it enhance the potential impact of leaders, it also serves to model appropriate relationships to leaders, staff and pupils.

> The general feature of human life that I want to evoke is its fundamentally *dialogical* character. We become full human agents, capable of understanding ourselves, and hence of defining an identity throughout acquisition of rich human languages of expression. [...] No one acquires the languages needed for self-definition on their own. We are introduced to them through exchanges with others who matter to us.
>
> **(Taylor, 1991: 33; original emphasis)**

People grow personally through their pivotal relationships, and also grow professionally through such relationships. However, the number of people that we engage with has a significant impact on the integrity and potential of these relationships – effective dialogue depends on quality and quantity. The potential significance and impact of dialogue is in inverse proportion to the number of people involved. Thus coaching, normally a one-to-one relationship, is probably the most significant and potentially successful strategy to support learning, personal change and growth. Five to seven participants seems to be the optimum number and after that the potential impact of dialogue is possibly diluted. In his study of human and animal interaction, Robin Dunbar argues that we live in what he calls 'circles of intimacy' that determine the regularity and depth of our relationships. The most significant circle is the innermost – usually a maximum of five people.

> "It seems that each of [our] circles of acquaintanceship maps quite neatly onto two aspects of how we relate to our friends. One is the frequency with which we contact them [...] But it also seems to coincide with the sense of intimacy we feel: we have the most intense relationships with the inner five.
>
> **(Dunbar, 2010: 33)**

This is a dimension of leadership that has not received the level of attention it needs or deserves. Leadership is usually at its most effective when it is relational rather than positional. One of the great strengths of dialogue is the potential it has to enhance relationships and secure engagement – an obvious example is the influence of coaches in sport.

Dialogue in leadership is a key resource to support a range of activities and desired outcomes, such as:

→ Developing shared understanding.

→ Using analytical techniques to identify problems and generate possible solutions.

→ Fostering a common language and shared vocabulary.

→ Enhancing the quality of decision making.

→ Working to build consensus.

→ Exposing fallacious and illogical arguments.

→ Boosting team effectiveness and productivity.

→ Questioning and challenging different perspectives.

Successful dialogue is a complex blend of art and science in that its success depends on elusive qualities such as trust and empathy. At the same time there are very clear protocols that inform the quality of outcome and process. A taxonomy of successful dialogue will include most of the following elements:

→ Mutual trust rooted in shared respect.

→ Empathy based on sensitivity to the needs of others.

→ Interdependent and collaborative working.

→ Commitment and engagement.

→ Appropriate questioning and challenge.

→ Feedback and reciprocity.

→ Recognition and reinforcement.

→ Humility and recognition of alternative perspectives.

→ Laughter.

→ Review to support improvement and consolidate success.

Above all, dialogue is a strategy to support personal learning and development through interactive and interdependent working such as lesson study. In this respect it is akin to Vygotsky's zone of proximal development (Vygotsky, 1978) – that is, learning potential is significantly enhanced through social interaction. In many ways it resembles the sort of learning that is found in action learning and joint practice development. The key to successful dialogue lies primarily in the quality of the questions asked and the challenges presented, and to the rigour of the dialectical process that seeks greater and greater clarity.

Many leadership teams have used the first *Leadership Dialogues* book as the basis for dialogue as part of their regular meeting cycle, and we would strongly endorse this use of leadership team time. However, it is worth stressing that while business meetings and leadership dialogues have much in common, successful team dialogue requires some specific elements to be in place, in particular:

→ A culture of challenge, analysis and reasoning.

→ Openness and inclusion.

→ Use of evidence where appropriate.

→ Recognition of the knowledge base available in the literature.

→ Translating principle into practice.

→ Taking action and working through practical projects.

→ Reviewing and reflecting on task and process.

Of course, it is the conversational dimension of dialogue that is the most significant element. However, it would be wrong to ignore the importance of review in terms of the focus of the conversation and the quality of the different aspects of the dialogic process. Essentially, the how is as least as important as the what. If senior leaders become confident and skilled at working through dialogue, then this can only be of benefit to their work with middle leaders and teachers – and so with pupils.

Securing equity and engagement

A   The education of vulnerable and disadvantaged pupils

Why is this an important topic for conversation?

One of the great challenges for those involved in any aspect of public service is to secure equality and equity, notably for the most vulnerable and disadvantaged. In essence, most education systems in the developed world have achieved equality – in that every child goes to school. However, it is true of many systems that not every child goes to a *good* school or that for many children the education system actually exacerbates their disadvantage by not providing appropriate compensatory interventions. Equity is essentially about fairness and social justice. Securing equity can be seen as the most fundamental component of school leadership and governance, and yet it remains elusive and problematic.

Key quotes for the section

> There is a growing body of evidence that shows that the highest-performing education systems are those that combine equity and quality. Equity in education is achieved when personal or social circumstances, such as gender, ethnic origin or family background, do not hinder achieving educational potential (fairness) and all individuals reach at least a basic minimum level of skills (inclusion).
>
> **(OECD, 2015: 31)**

1A

> " [E]quity is not the same as equal opportunity. When practiced in the context of education, equity is focused on outcomes and results and is rooted in the recognition that because children have different needs and come from different circumstances, we cannot treat them all the same.
>
> **(Noguera, 2008: xxvii)** "

Section discussion

Securing equity in education is both a moral imperative and a highly practical approach to governance, leadership and management. In many ways it can be seen as a test of the ability of leaders to translate policy into practice. It might be argued that the priority of some education systems has been quality, in terms of outcomes measured as academic excellence. Only in recent years has equity been seen as a significant factor.

In broad terms this is all about closing the gap. This is one of the crucial challenges for schools and government, and one that in England and other similar education systems remains stubbornly elusive. In England, the gap is usually understood as the difference in performance between pupils who are entitled to free school meals (FSM) and those who are not. In one of his final speeches as Her Majesty's Chief Inspector of Schools, Sir Michael Wilshaw made the following depressing observation:

> *The attainment gap between FSM and non-FSM secondary students hasn't budged in a decade. It was 28 percentage points 10 years ago and it is still 28 percentage points today. Thousands of poor children who are in the top 10% nationally at age 11 do not make it into the top 25% five years later. (Wilshaw, 2016)*

A key strategy for closing this gap has been the pupil premium, but evidence about its use seems to suggest that schools have not always followed the evidence available from the Education Endowment Foundation (EEF) Toolkit on Teaching and Learning.[1] Research has shown that 'Early intervention schemes, reducing class sizes, more one-to-one tuition and additional teaching assistants in the school were the most frequently cited priorities for the Pupil Premium'.[2] This is in spite of the fact that these approaches were rated as being less effective in terms of cost and impact.

---

1   See https://educationendowmentfoundation.org.uk/resources/teaching-learning-toolkit.
2   See https://www.nfer.ac.uk/publications/91062 and Cunningham and Lewis (2012).

Clearly, schools believe they are responding to research – in fact, 'More than half (52%) of the teachers said their school uses past experience of what works to decide which approaches and programmes to adopt to improve pupils' learning. Just over a third (36%) said their school looks at research evidence on the impact of different approaches and programmes' (ibid.).

Drawing on the NFER review of the strategies to support the education of disadvantaged pupils (Cunningham and Lewis, 2012) and the EEF toolkit, the following themes emerge as a basis for moving towards more equitable school based policies and interventions (Macleod et al., 2015):

1   A culture of high expectations and aspirations that apply to every aspect of the school's life and every member of the school community. In essence, the idea of the growth mindset applies to every dimension of school life – moving from 'I can't' to 'I can't *yet*'.

2   Securing engagement (see Section 1B).

3   Working towards consistently high teaching standards for all students – deploying the most effective teachers to the most disadvantaged groups.

4   Professional practice is evidence based in terms of accessing the research evidence to identify effective practice; developing a culture of professional enquiry across the school to review and improve practice; and ensuring that provision is informed by accurate and meaningful data.

5   Working towards personalised approaches for every student in order to optimise the relevance of their curriculum experience and the appropriateness of teaching and learning strategies. Crucially, providing choices that enhance the potential for engagement.

6   Leadership which secures that all of the above is consistent and equitable.

A crucial dimension of the leadership culture that is necessary to secure equity is a focus on middle leadership and, in particular, a strong sense of personal and collective accountability for the success of every individual. Middle leaders are essential to this process. A key theme of senior leadership and governance has to be the development of this culture across the school and the embedding of such accountability in the work of school governors, the leadership priorities of senior staff and the clarification of focus for middle leaders.

Equally significant is the development of a culture that is responsive to the actual involvement of pupils rather than relying only on adults' perceptions. This requires the detailed monitoring of pupil voice and the active involvement of pupils in the critical decisions that inform and influence their educational experiences.

With this in mind, three resources accompany this section. Resource 1A(i) enables you to obtain a real view of how your staff feel the key areas identified in the NFER review are progressing in your school. Resource 1A(ii) does the same for pupils. Resource 1A(iii) can be used to collate the results and focus priorities for the school.

Key questions

What do your school's aims or value statement say about fairness, equity and securing parity of esteem for all pupils?

When did you last audit the extent to which your principles on equity are reflected in practice?

What are the perceptions of your pupils and their parents?

To what extent are your strategies to close the gap (and spend pupil premium funding) based on reliable evidence?

Resources (Download)

1A(i)   Staff view on the school's implementation of strategies shown to help improve equity

1A(ii)   Pupil view on the school's implementation of strategies shown to help improve equity

1A(iii)   Summarising the school's implementation of strategies shown to help improve equity

B   Securing inclusion

Why is this an important topic for conversation?

Engagement is what makes the difference in terms of pupils getting the very best from their time at school and then realising their potential. Thinking about engagement in a holistic way, rather than in a piecemeal way, creates the possibility of understanding the factors that determine the extent to which pupils are fully committed to their own learning and are active members of the school community. In other words, inclusion!

Key quotes for the section

> The residents [of Sardinia] aren't blessed with extraordinary long lives because they drink the local red wine or eat plum tomatoes from their gardens ... ongoing face-to-face social contact with people who know and care about them matters more.
>
> **(Pinker, 2015: 60)**

> Of 64 studies of co-operative learning methods that provided group rewards based on the sum of members' individual learning, fifty (78%) found significantly positive effects on achievement and none found negative effects. Co-operative learning offers a proven practical means of creating exciting social and engaging classroom environments.
>
> **(Slavin, 2010: 170)**

Section discussion

Many of the tests of school effectiveness (e.g. Ofsted in England) take the various components of engagement as crucial evidence of effective leadership and management. For example:

> *Inspectors must spend as much time as possible gathering evidence about the quality of teaching, learning and assessment in lessons and other learning activities, to collect a range of evidence about the typicality of teaching, learning and assessment in the school. Inspectors will scrutinise pupils' work, talk to pupils about their work, gauging both their understanding and their engagement*

in learning, and obtain pupils' perceptions of the typical quality of teaching in a range of subjects. (Ofsted, 2016: 20)

The key issue for this section is that engagement is essentially about relationships: the individual's relationship with school, with teachers and their peers and, crucially, their personal sense of efficacy, value and the extent to which they view their future with hope and optimism.

Pupil engagement is the outcome of the interaction of a number of complex variables. Get the factors in the figure below as positives and engagement is almost certain; however, if they are negatives then it is very difficult to envisage situations where engagement will exist. We all know of the student who will only engage with one teacher or other adult in the school or who will truant from specific lessons but be in school without fail for others.

The Cambridge Primary Review define engagement as: 'To secure children's active, willing and enthusiastic engagement in their learning' (Alexander and Armstrong, 2010: 197). The components of such engagement are shown below.

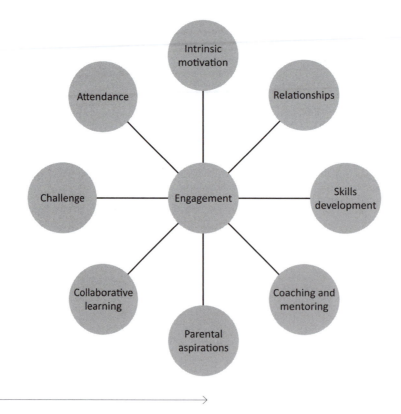

Intrinsic motivation

Intrinsic motivation is found in those students who have made a personal psychological commitment to their work. They are working because they want to rather than because they have to. They take pride in their work, often exceed expectations in terms of work and performance, and persist even when faced with challenges or obstacles. They value their involvement in the learning process for its own sake and welcome participation with others – their engagement is often infectious. According to Carol Dweck (2006), some people believe their success is based on innate ability; these individuals are said to have a 'fixed' theory of intelligence (fixed mindset). Others, who believe their success is based on having the opposite mindset, which involves hard work, learning, training and doggedness, are said to have a 'growth' or an 'incremental' theory of intelligence (growth mindset). Intrinsic motivation is also about self-efficacy, self-belief and a positive disposition that is essentially optimistic about personal potential.

Relationships

Relationships with other pupils and staff are based on high levels of mutual respect, trust and courtesy. Pupils feel safe and confident with each other and are supported in adopting strategies to develop emotional literacy and mature interactions.

Skills development

Challenge only engages to the extent that learners have the skills commensurate with the challenge, otherwise they are either bored or intimidated. Cognitive skills development of attributes such as analysing and synthesising, explaining and justifying, demonstrating causality and constructing a logical argument all have the potential to increase confidence, personal efficacy and therefore engagement.

Coaching and mentoring

Coaching is often seen as a panacea for most issues of engagement and development, and it is generally credited with being one of the most potent learning strategies. For feedback to make an impact on an individual's learning, potential achievement and possible success, the teacher/facilitator/coach has to focus on developing a growth mindset and fostering a relationship based on a balance of challenge and skills development, underpinned by high trust and a shared commitment to improvement.

Parental aspirations

It is almost impossible to exaggerate the importance of values and attitudes in determining pupil engagement. The implicit and explicit attitudes towards school and education in general are a crucial factor, especially in the early and primary years. Quite apart from parental influences on literacy and cognitive development, it is parental attitudes that influence a child's potential engagement.

Collaborative learning

Learning is a social process. While there is much that we can learn on our own in most situations, collaborative learning is often more effective in terms of understanding and application.

> Relaxed alertness is the optimal state of mind for meaningful learning. *People in a state of relaxed alertness experience low threat and high challenge. Essentially the learner is both relaxed and to some extent excited or emotionally engaged at the same time. This is the foundation for taking risks in thinking, questioning and experimenting, all of which are essential. In this state the learner feels competent and confident and has a sense of meaning and purpose. (Caine et al., 2009: 21; original emphasis).*

Challenge

Problem solving is the basis of all effective learning and we are at our most effective as learners when faced with a challenge, a problem to solve or an enquiry to follow. One way of understanding human development is to see it in terms of an increasing capacity to solve problems collaboratively. Challenge based approaches are the basis of most leisure activities and an essential component of the cognitive development of young people. Challenge in learning is a key element in securing engagement.

Attendance

Pupils are in school because it is required by law but they are also present in the sense of being actively involved in every aspect of the school day. They should be ready to learn and demonstrate enjoyment, excitement and enthusiasm when in school. They should also be a crucial role model for other, especially younger, pupils in terms of punctuality and involvement.

It might be helpful to see these eight elements as possible clauses in a learning contract. Their significance will vary according to the circumstances of the individual pupil, but in broad terms the more of the clauses that are positive, the higher the potential for engagement. The negative corollary applies equally significantly. So enhancing an individual's engagement requires personalised interventions based on shared diagnosis.

Key questions

Who in your school has leadership responsibility for student engagement as opposed to attendance and/or behaviour?

Does your school data indicate specific groups in the school who are particularly vulnerable in terms of disengagement?

Is there any correlation in your school between tedious, unimaginative and, frankly, boring teaching and pupil engagement?

Resources (Download)

1B(i)	Investigating the disengaged pupil
1B(ii)	Improving engagement

C   Combatting exclusion

Why is this an important topic for conversation?

In the same way that prison deprives an offender of his or her liberty – a basic component of a democratic society – so exclusion denies a young person of their right to be educated within mainstream provision. The seriousness of such a penalty should not be underestimated. Students who are in danger of exclusion are, by a range of criteria, some of the most vulnerable and disadvantaged. Their rights have to be balanced against the rights of their peers and staff to work in a safe and positive environment. It is a bit like *Lord of the Flies*, only without the desert island.

Key quotes for the section

> In the end, however, a disruptive boy's resistance has no effect on the value system that education establishes for children because, treated as an individual, the most disruptive boy is usually excluded from school and often claimed by the street. And so, for as long as failing schools are protected from proper scrutiny and disruptive boys are treated as individuals with emotional and behavioural difficulties, the basis of the formation of their peer groups is neglected as a social phenomenon, and the cycle goes on.
>
> **(Evans, 2006: 116)**

> This is the first time I have felt a school or its teachers actually see me – it is the first time I have actually felt valued. The first time I have believed that education has any connection to me.
>
> **(A pupil of Stone Soup Academy, an alternative provision free school)**

Section discussion

There is a somewhat bizarre contradiction, which students are quick to spot, in that the most serious sanction available to a school consists in denying a student access to the school. The second most serious sanction consists of requiring students to spend extra time in school. What is very clear is that there is an obvious link between exclusion and long term disaffection, sometimes resulting in criminal convictions and prison. Some

48% of young offenders in custody have a reading age at or below that of an 11-year-old (Clark and Dugdale, 2008: 5).

Experienced teachers know intuitively which students are most likely to be at risk of exclusion, but, more importantly, the data provides a well-defined profile of the students most likely to be excluded. Department for Education figures from 2013/2014 show that boys are over three times more likely to receive a permanent exclusion and almost three times more likely to receive a fixed period exclusion than girls. Pupils with special educational needs (SEN) (with and without statements) account for seven in ten of all permanent exclusions and six in ten of all fixed period exclusions. Pupils with SEN without statements have the highest permanent exclusion rate and are around nine times more likely to receive a permanent exclusion than pupils with no SEN. Pupils with statements of SEN have the highest fixed period exclusion rate and are around nine times more likely to receive a fixed period exclusion than pupils with no SEN. Pupils known to be eligible for and claiming free school meals are around four times more likely to receive a permanent or fixed period exclusion than those who are not eligible; this is similar to previous years. Of the total number of permanent exclusions, 81% occurred in secondary schools. Overall persistent disruptive behaviour is the most common reason for permanent exclusions, accounting for 32.7% of all permanent exclusions (DfE, 2015).

Use resource 1C(i) to analyse the permanent and temporary exclusions from your own school. Share this analysis with your team. Are you happy with the picture this data paints of your school?

On the premise that the most important overarching strategy is to develop interventions in order to pre-empt the behaviour that might lead to exclusion, on the basis that prevention is better than the cure, some of the following strategies might be appropriate:

→ Developing an early warning system to identify students with a propensity to behaviour that might lead to exclusion.

→ Ensuring that school rules, norms, codes of conduct and curriculum requirements are enforced with absolute consistency and that record keeping is scrupulous.

→ Developing a diagnostic approach in order to identify students with some of the following characteristics: rejection of school by parents; high intelligence but no engagement with school work; limited social skills; poor self-control; frustration at school norms expressed through anger; a potential for personal violence; boredom with the curriculum and learning experiences; conflict with teachers (e.g. personality clashes).

→ Appointing learning mentors to work with individuals and small groups on a daily basis to monitor behaviour, respond to any incidents and reinforce positive and successful behaviours.

→ Providing access to credible role models who have succeeded through the education system.

→ Developing high impact literacy interventions to enable meaningful and significant engagement with aspects of the curriculum, and ensuring that students are taught by the most effective teachers and senior staff.

→ Providing alternative learning experiences which will usually involve craft skills (e.g. repairing and refurbishing bicycles/playground equipment, renovating computers).

→ Building a strong sense of shared identity through positive social interaction and shared projects designed to secure commitment and engagement.

→ Making use of a wide range of multimedia approaches.

→ Working with teachers to ensure that lessons are genuinely differentiated to allow for success.

→ Adopting restorative practices that create a climate of fairness.

Use resource 1C(ii) to investigate the menu of strategies you are currently using and to identify areas needing further effort. Devise an action plan to make sure that in this crucial area your school bears no resemblance to *Lord of the Flies*, and that the balance is very clearly towards inclusion and not exclusion. It is important to extend this conversation as broadly as possible. Some staffrooms can be quick to call for the exclusion of a difficult pupil without fully considering the implication of such an action. The more staff understand the causes of behaviours which can lead to exclusion, the more likely these environments will not trigger them.

Key questions

> Is there a case for arguing that exclusion may be practically necessary but morally unacceptable?

> Is your school's approach to disruptive behaviour based on prevention rather than cure or sanction?

> How much time is spent listening to the most disruptive students in your school?

> How many of your staff have the skills needed to work with the most disruptive students?

Resources (Download)

1C(i) Analysing the exclusions in your school
1C(ii) Analysing the strategies to combat exclusion in your school

D   Transition and induction

Are you really serious about supporting successful movement between phases of schooling?

Why is this an important topic for conversation?

Each year around the world millions of young people move from one level of education to another. There is no set age for this to happen – we know of examples at 7, 9, 11, 12, 14, 15, 16 and 18 – but we are confident that if we keep looking we would find the complete set. In other words, there is no 'magic age' at which changing schools is a good idea. These are not neurologically based decisions but generally historical and practical ones. About the only thing that is persistently common between the procedures in each country is the fact that attainment and attitudinal dips are reported in the year following the transfer. Often these dips are never corrected. Too often the problem is seen as a natural process, but in a few countries is it regarded as a priority for action.

Key quotes for the section

> The nature of peer status changes too, as children go from being 'big fish in a small pool' to minnows in an uncharted ocean. As they adjust to the new environment, the new organisational arrangements, the new relationships and the new sets of rules (both explicit and hidden), there may be conflict between social and educational agendas.
>
> **(Jindal-Snape and Miller, 2008: 222)**

> While the primary (but not secondary) school played a small part in accounting for different transition experiences, controlling for a wide range of sociodemographic and other factors, personal characteristics were much more important. Respondents of lower ability and lower self-esteem experienced poorer school transitions ...
>
> **(West et al., 2010: 21)**

Section discussion

If transition is such a key issue for schools, how come so little emphasis seems to be placed on it? The factors are numerous but one of the simplest is probably a practical one – no one actually 'owns' the process. If you take a moment to consider the potential issues that would be caused by a hedge between two neighbours, which neither side owned, you begin to understand the stumbling blocks around the much more important process of transition. Around the world groups of teachers view their counterparts across the transition divide with scepticism and mistrust. Recriminations abound: 'What were they teaching at that school?' from one side; 'That child was wonderful with us – what have they done to him?' from the other.

We are sometimes contacted by schools that claim to have a 'good transition process'; sadly this is rarely the reality. Too often their self-perceived excellence is based on a few enthusiastic, high energy days in the summer ('transition days'). While we would be the first to agree that this is certainly a start, to believe that a few well-meaning days can address the multitudinous issues is naive. We would propose changing the names of such days to 'induction days' and focusing on beginning the process of 'inducting' pupils into their new school – for example, raising awareness of new faces, locations, timings and procedures. However, to begin addressing the many wider and more complex issues of learning, something much more involved is required.

So, when should effective transition begin? Half a year before the move? A full year before? We would suggest something much longer: thinking of the process of transition as the movement through the whole learning journey for each individual is a much more effective approach. In other words, we need to reduce the importance of the individual institution and increase the importance of the full educational experience. Imagine you were on a tour when halfway through you were passed to another guide – how would you feel if the two experiences seemed to lack continuity? If entire days appeared to go over the same ground? It is likely you would be calling for a refund, rightly expecting that the tour should be better coordinated. Sadly, too many young people feel this frustration and confusion, but without access to a complaints department!

If learning is actually a series of strands from infancy to adulthood, the actual location of delivery at any one point should be fairly irrelevant, and may even be different for any two individuals. Consider the benefits that could be gained by a 6-year-old studying some of their lessons along with older pupils and their teachers. The importance of this improved clarity around continuity can have far reaching effects on the way pupils think about their learning and view any shifts in its location.

Use resource 1D(i) to think about your own approach to transition. Analyse what proportion of your current activities are actually induction ones. If any activities do not fall into either category it may not mean it is without use, but in times of high demand on teacher and curriculum time it might be something to consider removing. Once this activity is completed, most school leadership teams may decide they want to increase the amount of long term transition events in their school. However, in an already packed curriculum, the need to focus these activities strategically becomes clear.

Perhaps the quote from West et al. (2010) gives clues to the priorities we should have. Have you ever identified the long term effect of transition in your own school from the point of view of your pupils? When teachers seek pupils' views on transition the focus often tends to be immediate and quite subjective. It might be advisable to try to identify pupils whose assessment and attendance hint at a deterioration since the move – resource 1D(ii) is designed to support this. Use this to analyse pupils who you believe may not be fulfilling their potential since transition. Once you have identified them use 1D(iii) to help find out key aspects of concern from these pupils. Try to pinpoint areas in which they didn't feel as if learning was a journey.

Avoid the temptation to be defensive over issues raised by pupils; instead, try to isolate the top three areas that could be improved. Once you have these priorities, consider them as a problem to be solved across the full educational journey and not just in your school. Make sure both sides of the transition divide engage in trying to improve the matter. For example, if major differences in teaching and learning style in maths are identified, first determine if the differences are necessary and, if so, attempt to smooth out the process.

If transition could be depicted like this:

Attempt to make the change more like this:

It is essential that the process of learning develops as a child matures, but to assume this is a linear process directly linked to age is inappropriate. While for some pupils (maybe you were one of them) the process of transition is an enjoyable adventure, for too many it is the beginning of a disconnect with education.

Key questions

In the first quote Jindal-Snape and Miller describe a possible 'conflict between social and educational agendas'. How does this relate to current experiences in your school? What evidence do you have?

Would you describe your own school's activities as being more of a programme of transition or induction?

'Some nerves are good – helps stop them getting too big for their boots. After all, transition didn't do me any harm,' said one teacher recently. Discuss.

Can you identify which pupils have been negatively affected by current procedures for transition in your school?

Resources (Download)

1D(i)   Induction or transition: analysing the activities of two schools serving different age groups

1D(ii)   Identifying pupils who may be negatively impacted by transition

1D(iii) Questions for pupils about transition

E   Balancing achievement and vulnerability

Why is this an important topic for conversation?

School leaders across the world are reporting increased pressure to achieve high assessment scores for all their pupils, while at the same time recognising that levels of pupil vulnerability are rising. These two external forces appear to be at odds. It can be tempting for school leaders to respond to this dilemma by labelling it as a 'national issue'; in this section we consider how leadership teams can ensure it is a 'local issue' – one they are actively seeking to solve.

Key quotes for the section

> As children move through the school system, emotional and behavioural wellbeing become more important in explaining school engagement, while demographic and other characteristics become less important.
>
> **(Gutman and Vorhaus, 2012: 3)**

> This isn't a school; it's a family, a social services department, and the rest. If we're going to improve on education, these other things have got to be dealt with.
>
> **(head teacher, The Farcliffe School, quoted in Lupton, 2004: 23)**

> Given the remarkable success that special schools (and, lest we forget, nurseries and pupil referral units) have achieved (as indicated by Ofsted's inspection outcomes) [...] why isn't this headline news?
>
> **(O'Brien, 2016: 63)**

> These results suggest strongly that parental divorce can be a critical event in the academic development of children.
>
> **(Mulholland et al., 1991: 268)**

Section discussion

If we consider vulnerable to mean being 'exposed to the possibility of being attacked or harmed, either physically or emotionally',[3] it is perhaps not a surprise that schools feel there are more vulnerable pupils than there were a generation ago. First, we now have a much wider definition of vulnerability and an increased awareness and sensitivity as a result of this. Second, the advent of social media has resulted in many more ways for the vulnerable to be targeted and exploited. This double effect is then intensified by an increasingly litigious society, where 'blame' always needs to be placed at someone's door; increasingly this 'someone' is within an education or social care setting – 'Why did no one do anything?' When the increased accountability/outcomes approach to education (which is starting to dominate around the globe) is added to this worrying mix, we are in danger of being pushed into quick, superficial answers.

Most educationalists instinctively believe that if a child is experiencing physical or mental harm they will not be as focused (or as successful) in their learning – 'If Julie is having to undergo that most evenings, why on earth would she be interested in photosynthesis?' This attitude is understandable, and to an extent is backed up by research (e.g. Duncan and Murnane, 2011). However, is this attitude helpful for the child involved? Does it help them to maximise their potential? Or does it merely allow a stereotype to become true? Recognising that a child is vulnerable is clearly a vital step in providing them with support, but the next stage is probably the most important in their learning: 'What happens now?'

Perhaps clues to the next steps lie in the quote from special school head teacher Jarlath O'Brien, who points out that an unusually high number of special schools and referral units have been identified as outstanding over recent years. In other words, perhaps the schools that know most of their pupils are vulnerable have a more successful approach to their learning.

Certainly, insights into the day-to-day workings of a highly regarded pupil referral unit give hints as to the reasons for their success: they seek to offer a unique curriculum for every child; they have one-to-one coaching sessions at regular intervals; they try to relate as much of the learning as possible to future work opportunities; they focus on active and engaging teaching methods; they try to make the school feel 'untypical'; they produce an environment that feels safe; they aim to produce an 'I can do it' attitude towards achievement; and they appear to balance a caring and supportive environment with one of high expectations.

---

3   See https://en.oxforddictionaries.com/definition/vulnerable.

Use resource 1E(i) to look at your own school through the eyes of the vulnerable learner. How do you approach your learners and what does this tell them about your attitude towards them?

Perhaps the most important aspect of the success of special schools is the personalisation of the high expectations asked of pupils. Many young people feel 'done to' by the school system, but vulnerable children may have a greatly heightened distrust of the adults in their lives. One vulnerable child described how she 'knew' the only reason the school wanted her to get better GCSE grades was to improve the school's own reputation. Young people are growing up in a world where politicians are openly ridiculed for their blatant electioneering, so we should not be surprised that many pupils doubt the motives of those who provide their education.

Dialogues with vulnerable children are complex and should always be carefully considered, but that doesn't mean they shouldn't be held. Resource 1E(ii) is offered as a non-threatening opening into a conversation around ways to improve the well-being of pupils in your school. Give the sheet to any pupil who you think would have a different perspective; once they have completed it give them the opportunity to explain it to you.

In this area, neuroscience and leadership theory are aligned: if you want a child to succeed they must feel that they can trust those doing the educating, and be given trust in return. The school may not always be able to remove the threats to the child outside the building, but they can make the learning experience within the school a more positive and open one.

Key questions

What is your definition of vulnerability?

What do you actually do when you identify vulnerability?

Are vulnerable children nurtured or challenged (or both)?

How are levels of openness and trust within your school?

What is it like to be a vulnerable child at your school?

Resources (Download)

1E(i)	Looking at your approach to vulnerable learners
1E(ii)	What I really think about my school

Clarifying the purpose of education

A   What does it mean to be educated?

Why is this an important topic for conversation?

The quality of an education system is fundamental to the development of a socially stable, economically sound and democratically secure society. Education is a major beneficiary of taxation and its practitioners ought to be accountable for the effectiveness of their stewardship. At the same time there is a need to recognise and respect the professional knowledge and expertise of education professionals, in the same way that doctors and lawyers are accorded distinctive status. Education can never be a value-free activity – every aspect of decision making about the nature of schooling, the content of the curriculum and the role of education in society is open to debate.

There is a very strong case for arguing that school leadership has a superordinate function in developing a consensus around the core issues about the nature and purpose of the education process as translated into practice in a particular context.

Key quotes for the section

> Where there is no vision, the people perish.
>
> **(Proverbs 29:18)**

> How do we conceive learning? Is it always a 'means' to arrive at some 'end', preconceived by 'the system'?
>
> That surely does not fit the *informal* learning whereby children adapt to new circumstances, internalise what is experienced, come to see things differently through interactions with others, seek to understand what is puzzling, reconceptualise the world tentatively in the light of experience. They are learning what they become – 'that is the human condition'.
>
> **(Pring, 2013: 32; original emphasis)**

> [S]chools will almost certainly wish to advance some values and principles above others. The exercise of defining aims for a national education system, then, is ethical and political, and all such aims are by their nature contestable. Far from being a matter of 'mere common sense' as generations of politicians would have us believe, education is, fundamentally, a moral pursuit.
>
> **(Alexander and Armstrong, 2010: 175)**

Section discussion

A more accurate translation of 'perish' in the line from Proverbs is 'unrestrained', 'lack focus' or 'lack cohesion'. It has become a truism that one of the defining characteristics of successful leadership is the ability to articulate a vision for the future and then to build a consensus around that vision in order to clarify and focus the key priorities of the organisation. There seems to be a significant correlation between organisational effectiveness and clarity of purpose. Indeed, most recruitment strategies are built around the extent to which candidates are committed to the purpose and values of the organisation they are seeking to join.

It is probably the case that one of the characteristics of high performing schools and education systems is a significant degree of agreement about what the vision is. In other words, clarification and agreement about 'the business we are in'. It may be significant that two of the historically very successful education systems in Europe – those of Finland and the Netherlands – are characterised by a high degree of consensual authoritarianism. Both societies have very clear views on the values and norms that govern daily social interactions, and the majority of the population observe and enforce these assumptions. The same appears to be true of sports teams, military units and highly effective teams in almost any context.

The challenge for education professionals is that there is very little consensus in most societies as to the nature and purpose of education. Indeed, in England, a range of very different perspectives have been the prevailing orthodoxy for a time and then abandoned. A further challenge is who actually determines the nature of the education process and defines the appropriate outcomes and the means of assessing their successful accomplishment. In England, it is probably true to say that teachers 'owned' education until James Callaghan's Ruskin College speech in 1976 opened the debate about the ownership and development of the curriculum. Since then, and particularly since the advent of the Blair government in 1997, education has increasingly been subject to control by central government, with an implicit rather than an explicit view of the nature and purpose of education.

One of the major issues with leadership in education is the lack of a consensus about the nature of the educational process, with significant tensions emerging from the resulting ambiguity. It might be naive to even propose the need for any sort of hegemony around the nature of education. As with debates around defence, health care and social provision, there is no absolute truth; the important thing is to participate in the debate and be able to make confident choices when a choice is available.

In very broad terms, the answer to the question about what it means to be educated has multiple possible permutations, most of which will include some of the following in varying degrees of significance:

→ An educated person is someone who is a confident learner with a range of intellectual and social skills and the confidence to follow their own path in life.

→ Higher education institutions and employers request that schools prepare pupils specifically for them.

→ Education is about creating citizens who are committed to living in a democratic society rooted in the rule of law and acceptance of diversity.

→ Schools exist to prepare young people for adult life by developing the knowledge and skills necessary to participate in society.

→ Educational outcomes are to be measured in terms of spiritual, social, cultural and environmental awareness.

→ Education is essentially a moral process designed to equip young people with the confidence to make wise choices about their lives.

→ An educated person is an academically successful person who achieves the standards defined by government, employers, higher education and society.

→ The core purpose of education is to secure well-being and happiness.

These options are perhaps best seen as the ingredients in a recipe. Which ingredients are selected will have a significant effect on the final outcome, but almost more important is the ratio – which can profoundly influence the nature of the outcome. It is unlikely that anyone would argue for the dominance of one of these factors to the exclusion of others; equally, some factors will always have a distinctive status irrespective of context or time.

The final point to be made is that educational purposes and priorities change over time. By definition the future is unknowable, but there are enough clues to allow us to be reasonably confident in identifying trends and issues that may point to a significant rethinking of some of the basic assumptions that inform our current thinking. In essence, some new ingredients may become available as others disappear. For example, there seems to be little doubt that information technology and environmental issues will assume increasing significance, as will the fact that prevailing models are not delivering in terms of social justice and social mobility.

Key questions

How does your school define an educated person?

To what extent is that definition shared by your pupils, their parents, and teachers and governors?

How was the definition developed – to what extent is it distinctive to the school?

How is the definition reflected in the way your school functions on a day-to-day basis?

How are the basic assumptions about the nature of your school reviewed and updated?

Resources (Download)

2A(i)	Looking at your own views on the purpose of education
2A(ii)	Comparing views across the leadership team
2A(iii)	Investigating the team's views on education

B   Balancing the academic and the personal

Why is this an important topic for conversation?

This section focuses on the key education debate being held in almost every corner of the globe: what is education for? Is the main purpose of education to increase the academic knowledge of its citizens or to develop the desirable characteristics and aptitudes of the individual? Or, as many would suggest, a complex balance of the two?

Key quotes for the section

> We frequently attempt to prepare people for the future by imparting the wisdom gleaned from our own experiences. Sometimes our efforts are rewarded, but we are often less successful than we would like to be.
>
> **(Vosniadou and Ortony, 1989: 470)**

> Raising standards in education certainly seems like a good idea. There's no point in lowering them. But standards of what? Why do we choose them and how do we implement them?
>
> **(Robinson and Aronica, 2015: 18)**

> For some time now discussion on education has been dominated by a language of test scores and economic competitiveness. To be sure, a major goal of [...] education is to prepare the young to make a living. But parents send their kids to school for many other reasons as well: intellectual, social, civic, ethical, aesthetic. Historically, these justifications for schooling have held more importance. Not today.
>
> **(Rose, 2014: 4)**

Section discussion

We all want to live in a country with an excellent education system; to suggest otherwise is nonsensical. The problem is how we define this 'excellence'. As the section title suggests, and the quotations demonstrate, the answer may be approached from an academic perspective, from a character perspective or from a hybrid of the two.

If our only filter for this question is an academic one, then surely the answer becomes more straightforward: does our school score the highest test marks? But, wait a moment … does the test measure knowledge or memory? Is the test fair? Can only a set number pass? What if the starting level of kids in our area was different? The questions pour out and place in doubt what seemed a logical approach. If comparing things that appear intrinsically 'measurable' is difficult, how on earth can we consider comparing things that seem more ethereal or vague, such as character and personality?

So, is the root of the problem the current obsession with comparing education systems? Any attempt to decide if one system is better than the other gives us the same problem faced by popular TV car shows. In these programmes, various car experts routinely argue about the respective merits of select examples from similar classes of cars. Few question the rationale behind the method. The presenters compare the vehicles from a variety of different perspectives: comfort, handling, fuel economy, looks and so on. It is not unusual to find one car excelling in a particular test while performing worse in another. 'It's not just about the numbers!' one presenter will then exclaim. The upshot is quite often a split decision with the conclusion being that the 'best car' is in the eye of the beholder.

It is unlikely that governments around the world will be rushing to emulate this approach in education. With over 4% of GDP (typically) being committed to education, it is not a surprise that politicians want to show that taxpayers' money is being spent effectively. They want to find a simple measure to point to that backs up the success of their policies, a simple tick box that shows their schools are good. This is one of the main drivers in the rise of academic comparisons and explains the current fascination with PISA league tables.

Are you happy with the focus in your own school? (Or do you feel you are a spacious family saloon car being judged on your ability to park in small spaces?) The reality is that you may have limited traction on national policy, but you can begin to change the debate within your own school. This is where national attitudes can begin to be shifted.

What are the drivers in your school? What are the reasons you all get out of bed in the morning? If you were able to compare a child before their time at your school with them at the end of their schooling, what would be the biggest changes you would see? Which changes are you most proud of? Use resource 2B(i) to capture your thinking. Try to distil the essence of the main changes you bring about – things that probably would not happen without your work.

Do you celebrate these successes within your school? It can feel disheartening to work in a school that appears fixated on results alone. Use resource 2B(ii) to develop a car inspired advert for the work you do in your school. Consider the balance you have between the data and the personal growth you bring about. Whether you use this resource or a method of your own choosing, don't underestimate the benefit that can be found by celebrating the successes you achieve. Too many teachers feel they are 'failing' because the academic data for their pupils is not as high as in some other schools. If the fixation with test achievement is allowed to remain unchallenged within the school, there is little chance of the national debate on the topic being shifted either. Everyone wants their pupils to perform as well as possible in any tests, but this should not be the defining goal of our schools.

Key questions

What do you think education is for?

Do you ever discuss this in your school?

What do you think is the main role of your school?

Do you have a balanced approach to the aims at your school?

Resources (Download)

2B(i)   Thinking around the changes in the personal development of your pupils
2B(ii)   A 'car advert blank' to be used internally to celebrate the positive aspects of your school

C   Securing every child's entitlement

Why is this an important topic for conversation?

If education is one of a number of basic rights in a democratic society to be judged in terms of equality and equity, then it is important to define what benefits and outcomes should accrue from living in such a society. For educational leaders, it is important to be able to place education in context and recognise its potential contribution to a child's entitlement. This discussion is therefore concerned with the child as a person, not as a pupil, and therefore the discussion also needs to address issues of well-being and happiness.

Key quotes for the section

> Intellectual and socioemotional development are inextricably intertwined from an early age. Research has shown that so-called noncognitive skills (grit, social sensitivity, optimism, self-control, conscientiousness, emotional stability) are very important for life success. They can lead to greater physical health, school success, college enrollment, employment and lifetime earnings, and can keep people out of trouble and out of prison. These skills are at least as important as cognitive skills in predicting such measures of success and may be even more important in our postindustrial future than in the preindustrial and industrial past.
>
> **(Putnam, 2015: 111)**

> Wellbeing serves as a double duty. It directly supports literacy and numeracy; that is, emotional health is strongly associated with cognitive achievement. It also is indirectly but powerfully part of the educational and societal goal of dealing with the emotional and social consequences of failing and being of low status. In this sense political leaders must have an explicit agenda of wellbeing, of which education is one powerful component.
>
> **(Fullan, 2006: 46)**

> Good parents guide and shape; they don't smother. The same applies to schools, which build resilience in their students not by sheltering them but by exposing them to challenges. Step by step, they learn that they can overcome difficulties and, in doing so, they build inner grit and strength.
>
> **(Seldon, 2015: 240)**

Section discussion

One way of understanding a child's entitlement is to be very clear about what needs should be met across the spectrum of the personal, the social and the moral. The debate is focused on agreeing what the needs are, how they might be prioritised and who is responsible for securing them. There appears to be an overwhelming consensus that parents have the primary responsibility, but we all know of cases where parenting is inadequate or inappropriate. The tragic manifestation is the high number of children who die as a result of neglect or violence and the subsequent public inquiry finds that everybody and nobody was responsible.

At its most fundamental, a child's entitlement is probably best summarised in terms of well-being, although this remains an elusive concept with no clear consensus across the various agencies as to what it actually means. As a starting point for this discussion, therefore, it might be helpful to consider what needs have to be met in order to achieve well-being and so identify all the elements that might be included in any definition of a child's entitlement. There is a very clear and causal relationship between pupil well-being and academic performance – in essence, positive well-being leads to positive performance.

One way of understanding this issue is to use a model such as Maslow's (1943) hierarchy of needs, while recognising that the relative significance of each dimension will vary according to age and social and economic circumstances, and also that the model is culturally problematic in that it is essentially individualistic. It is also worth exploring the fact that the traditional hierarchy of needs is not universal. For many people in advanced societies the emphasis on physiological needs and safety does not have the same level of significance as in many developing societies, as these requirements can usually be taken as given, although that can change very rapidly as countless recent refugee crises demonstrate. On this basis, the traditional hierarchy has been inverted and modified to reflect the possible components of a child's entitlement.

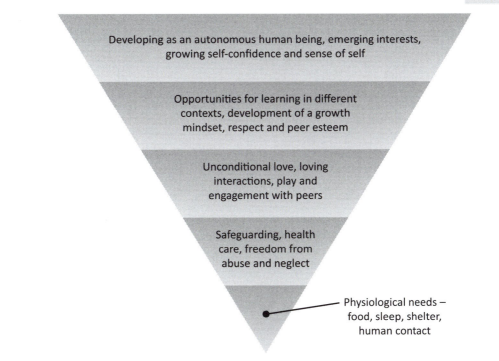

Developing as an autonomous human being, emerging interests, growing self-confidence and sense of self

Opportunities for learning in different contexts, development of a growth mindset, respect and peer esteem

Unconditional love, loving interactions, play and engagement with peers

Safeguarding, health care, freedom from abuse and neglect

Physiological needs – food, sleep, shelter, human contact

At the most basic level, a child's entitlement can be expressed as a good night's sleep (e.g. 10 hours for a 9-year-old) followed by a healthy breakfast and a safe journey to school. At the highest level, it is about recognising and respecting special needs, supporting particular talents and creating an environment that fosters growth, social confidence and competence. The most challenging element of this model is possibly the idea of unconditional love, but perhaps that should be regarded as the superordinate entitlement:

> [B]eing a parent is like making a garden. It's about providing a rich, stable, safe environment that allows many different kinds of flowers to bloom. It's about producing a robust, flexible ecosystem that lets children themselves create many varied, unpredictable kinds of adult futures. It is also about a specific human relationship, a committed, unconditional love, between a specific parent and a specific child. (Gopnic, 2016: 233)

Use this quote and resource 2C(i) to have a dialogue about the level of entitlement currently in your school.

Given the emphasis on performativity across a very narrow range of highly instrumental outcomes, which in some respects now dominates certain aspects of schooling, there is clearly a potential tension between the assessment of academic/curriculum outcomes and a holistic model of well-being based on the personal and the social. Strategies to secure entitlement through an emphasis on well-being include:

→ Auditing current levels of well-being and issues around mental health.

→ Reviewing the school value statement and aims/mission to focus explicitly on well-being and happiness for all members of the school community.

→ Identifying the development of well-being as a key outcome for all pupils.

→ Embedding references to well-being and happiness in all school policies and strategies (not through a separate policy).

→ Rethinking personal, social, health and economic (PSHE) education and pastoral care in terms of well-being and engagement (see section 1B).

→ Identifying well-being champions across the school – governors, members of the senior leadership team (SLT), teachers, support staff and pupils. Focusing pupil voice on well-being.

→ Providing training for all staff on well-being related issues.

→ Cultivating a culture of prevention rather than cure; introducing strategies to build resilience and confidence.

→ Developing links with appropriate agencies (e.g. Mind).

→ Monitoring the full range of entitlement based outcomes and incorporating them into the annual review cycle.

Use resource 2C(i) to provoke discussion in your school around these strategies.

Key questions

How confident are you that your school is securing every child's entitlement?

How is that entitlement expressed in terms of school policies and strategies?

What preventative strategies do you have in place? How effective are they?

What role do the pupils play in securing their entitlement?

How are parents and the wider community involved in developing a holistic view of educational outcomes?

What opportunities does your school's curriculum offer for the development of personal qualities and well-being as identified previously in this section?

Resources (Download)

2C(i)   Evaluating the hierarchy of needs in your school
2C(ii) Investigating entitlement in your school

D   Building consensus across the school community

Why is this an important topic for conversation?

The power of the group vs. the power of the individual. Consensus has the potential to transform hundreds of disparate voices into a single one. It may not be an easy goal to achieve, and once reached it is easy to lose. It is not hard to spot a school where there is widespread agreement on aims and a common understanding of the school's 'reason for being' because the energy, productivity and relationships combine to form a captivating atmosphere. There is no magic wand to create this type of school environment, but this section will give you some pointers on your journey towards it.

Key quotes for the section

> An environment where people spend a significant amount of their time affects their psyche and their behaviour. An organisation's climate encompasses values, communication and management styles, rules and regulations, ethical practices, reinforcement of caring behaviors, support for academic excellence, and characteristics of the physical environment.
>
> **(Orpinas and Horne, 2009: 49)**

> If the ethos or 'atmosphere' of a school is seen as exercising a more powerful influence on the behaviour and learning of school pupils than any single variable, then perhaps it is this over-riding spirit or tone which itself should be the focus for any intervention.
>
> **(Stratford, 1990: 183)**

Section discussion

When visitors talk of a recent visit to a school they will sometimes say, 'I could tell this was wonderful (or awful) from the moment I arrived at reception.' This does not indicate that the visitor was psychic or arrived pre-loaded with opinions, but that they detected the atmosphere from the first interactions they observed. When a visitor receives consistent messages from a variety of stimuli, they assume this is because the school has a common ethos – a consensus of attitude among all staff and pupils. This cohesion 'makes sense' to everyone in the building and elicits a positive response in the visitor. A school where attitudes seem to be in conflict produces the opposite response – one of negativity or unease. Some inspectors/consultants will use this phenomenon to form a judgement on the 'health' of a school.

Using a simple form like resource 2D(i), the views of a cross-section of people who work in the school (e.g. teachers, leaders, assistants and administrative staff) are collected, focusing on positive, non-threatening questions. It will quickly become clear if employee relationships within the school have a single positive thread or are the source of disharmony. It may be tempting for a member of the leadership team to attempt this task; however, an internal survey is much less likely to produce as honest a picture as an external one.

Once any lack in cohesion is identified, a mature leadership team will not see this as a threat ('Why don't they do as we tell them to?') but as an opportunity to move things forward ('How do we build a greater consensus?'). The challenge is how. It is not simply a case of stating, 'Hey guys, you all need to believe this!' What is your school looking for consensus around? If you decide that the drive is to produce 'aligned attitudes towards the school ethos/climate', this still lacks clarity. Is the school ethos what it says on the brochure or what happens in every interaction during a typical day?

One route to addressing this issue is to subdivide the concept of ethos into categories and investigate these separately. Using the quote from Orpinas and Horne (2009) as a starting point, we have values, communication, management/leadership styles, rules and regulations, ethical practices, reinforcement of caring behaviours, support for academic excellence and the physical environment. While this list is not exhaustive it seems a good place to begin developing your approach to improving consensus. Using resource 2D(ii), discuss the current state of the climate in your school. For each subdivision use the prompts to develop an accurate picture of the way things are on a typical day. Encourage all members of the leadership team to complete the form and then focus a meeting around this. Try to gain agreement in the group on the key successes and challenges in the creation of a positive and supportive climate. Try to prioritise the three most successful areas of climate – the ones where you believe you have the greatest positive impact. Note these on resource 2D(iii), for each one highlighting ways that this can be further celebrated and even greater staff cohesion created around them. Now identify the three areas that you agree are the weakest in the school climate at the moment. Write these on resource 2D(iv), for each one identifying ways this can be improved and how staff can be encouraged to work together.

To a certain extent, the clearer a school is able to express its vision and ethos, the more likely it is the staff will develop a consensus towards achieving it. When staff express views like, 'I don't know what that lot want of me,' it may be an example of diverting responsibility, but equally it may be a result of confused attitudes among the leadership team. Whatever your own particular religious opinions/beliefs, it is interesting to consider the relative success of church schools in many countries. Is it simply a factor of demographics? Or does the prominence of a 'church ethos', which is central to the daily life of the school, facilitate increased staff cohesion and consensus? If you are a secular organisation we are not suggesting that you carry out a mass 'conversion', but it may be worth visiting church schools in areas similar to your own and looking at the prominence (and consistency) of vision and ethos that you observe. It may be possible to mimic some of the attitudes and behaviours in your own school.

Key questions

How do all staff answer the question, 'Why are we here?'

Do you have a clear ethos and climate?

Is this expressed as clearly as it could be?

How could your vision be more clearly stated?

How do you ensure increased staff consensus around this vision?

Resources (Download)

2D(i)	Collecting the opinions of the staff
2D(ii)	Promoting debate around the current climate in your school
2D(iii)	Collating and developing the top three areas of strength
2D(iv)	Collating and improving the three weakest areas

E   The great education debate – what is it for?

Why is this an important topic for conversation?

Even if you have carried out the work in section 2D and produced a cohesive staff team with a real consensus around the vision for your school, this on its own is not enough. If the pupils, parents and governors of your school do not share, or possibly even agree with, your philosophy and direction of travel, then you have a serious issue in need of a solution.

Key quotes for the section

> If schooling is to play a part in transforming society, it has to be offered the chance to do it as a respected influence with a serious contribution to make rather than a mere tool of national politicians. If building character is part of the challenge for schools, along with raising horizons, encouraging positive lifestyles and broadening experience, then we have to promote this as a serious agenda rather than see it as an add-on or an imperative in crisis.
>
> **(Waters, 2013: 16)**

> [T]he wise school realises that the most powerful messages from adults about a school get carried through the local community by those who work there. So it is midday supervisors, the school's secretary, the learning assistant and the meals staff who are more likely to carry the reputation of the school than heads of department.
>
> **(Brighouse and Woods, 1999: 151)**

> The blame sometimes placed on schools for failing to redress all the negative impacts of poverty, for example, is entirely unfair and highly demotivating to good educators. [...] If our basic social institutions are highly unequal, then we must expect that inequality to show up in educational outcomes as well.
>
> **(Levin, 2008: 51)**

Section discussion

It is a natural human phenomenon that we judge our current situation through the lens of those we have experienced in the past. So it should not be a shock that many parents' expectations of their child's school will be influenced by their own experience of schooling. There was a time when the main function of schools was simply to provide the basic skills required to fit into a local, lifelong occupation. The requirements are now far more complex. The concept of a single career for life has diminished with the number of new roles increasing every year. The belief that the skills required for a role can be the end target for 12 years of schooling becomes nonsensical when you are considering a job that hasn't been invented yet! The principle of a local school for a local market has also vanished with the introduction of digitally connected citizens who can fulfil a job in a country many thousands of miles away, possibly communicating in a language other than their own. To propose a curriculum even loosely based on that of the previous century could be considered to be verging on the insane. As the quote from Mick Waters suggests, the demands on schools increase every year, both from politicians and the communities in which they are located.

In the name of democracy, many societies are giving more power in schools to parents. This can be both a positive and negative development. Some parents will be only too well aware of the changing world from their own experiences, and these parents may have a very strong desire to change the nature of education. Meanwhile, another group may be demanding for a return to the type of education championed during their own youth. This poses a dilemma for schools: do they ignore one set of parents, or do they try to please both? There is real danger in ignoring any parents, especially when the right-wing media still presents stories which fan the fire of traditionalists.

Perhaps the best approach is to begin a debate within the school and its community about what they think education is for. This discussion should include voices from as many different parts of the school community as possible. Make it clear that you want to hear people's views and ensure that you explain why the debate is needed. (There are many useful prompt videos on YouTube or similar online platforms – e.g. EF Explore America's 'What is 21st Century Education?' (2012).) Encourage people to accept that we need to think about our schools in a different way. One approach to really emphasise this is to collect media stories from the past month of the type, 'Increased divorce figures – schools need to do more work on relationships' or, 'Gun crime figures rise – schools need to develop teaching on dangers associated with it'. Set these demands alongside the latest requirements for improvements in examination results and pose the question, 'What do you (parents, pupils, governors) want us to prioritise in our school?'

Another way to encourage debate would be to present an alternative view of what 'good schooling' might look like. Resource 2E(i) provides a series of self-evaluation questions from Ian Gilbert (2013), requiring you to 'judge the success' of your own school. By considering the questions in respect to your school, the debate of 'core purpose' is placed at the centre. Used in conjunction with resources 2E(ii) (parents), 2E(iii) (governors) and 2E(iv) (pupils), the 'good school' scorecard can be used to move the conversation, and your school, forward. Take the results of each survey and publish them for your whole community to see – 'This is what we think!'

If you get strong messages from your school community, then make sure these are promoted loudly. Any future visits/inspections of your school should be carried out within this context. Some schools have even promoted their own self-analysis checklist on their website and made this a central demonstration of who they are. In light of the Ben Levin quote, referring to the work in section 2D should really help all your staff to develop a common approach to the work in the school.

Key questions

What is the reason for your school's existence?

What do parents expect of your school?

What do pupils want from your school?

What do governors expect from your school?

How can you move to greater consistency across all these groups?

2E

Resources (Download)

2E(i)	The 'good school' scorecard
2E(ii)	Parent survey – what do we want from our school?
2E(iii)	Governor survey – what do we want from our school?
2E(iv)	Pupil survey – what do we want from our school?

Middle leadership – the engine room of the school

A   Subject leadership

Why is this an important topic for conversation?

There is a clear and direct link between the quality of teaching and learning and the quality of leadership; indeed, it could be argued that the defining characteristic of leadership in education is securing effective learning. Equally, leadership needs to be understood not so much in terms of personal status but rather collective capacity. This is what Leithwood et al. (2006) refer to as 'total leadership' – that is, the potential for leadership that exists across the school. This might be thought of as leadership capital, in the same way that we think about social capital in a community or financial capital in a business. Clearly, the greater the level of capital, the greater the potential for high performance.

Key quotes for the section

> High quality middle leadership is about more than managing a subject or an aspect of school life. Middle leaders are enthusiasts for their subject, good managers and administrators – but to be truly effective they embrace the more challenging characteristics of leadership, which are to do with vision, strategy and a drive towards improvement.
>
> **(Cladingbowl, 2013: 6)**

3A

> Middle leaders have more day-to-day impact on standards than head teachers. Middle leaders are, simply, closer to the action. Teachers' and pupils' experience of leadership comes most frequently from their middle leaders.
>
> **(Russell Hobby, General Secretary, National Association of Head Teachers, quoted in Nelson and Quinn, 2016: 3)**

> Middle leaders, the engine room of the school, sit at the heart of this drive [to improve the quality of teaching inside each school]. They lead teams of teachers – turning senior leadership's strategy into outstanding classroom practice on a daily basis. They are closer to the action than senior leaders. High-performing middle leaders drive consistent teacher quality in their areas of responsibility.
>
> **(Toop: 2013)**

> The effects of high-quality teaching are especially significant for pupils from disadvantaged backgrounds: over a school year, these pupils gain 1.5 years' worth of learning with very effective teachers, compared with 0.5 years with poorly performing teachers. In other words, for poor pupils the difference between a good teacher and a bad teacher is a whole year's learning.
>
> **(Sutton Trust, 2011: 2)**

Section discussion

For most schools, the practical manifestation of learning-centred leadership is the creation of a leadership structure that distinguishes the various roles of leaders in terms of governance, strategic leadership, leadership of subjects/middle leadership, leadership in the classroom and student leadership/pupil voice.

Subject leadership is particularly significant because the evidence is quite unequivocal that the single most powerful factor in securing consistently excellent education is the quality of subject teaching. It therefore follows that the focus of leadership should be primarily on the quality of teaching and learning, and for middle leaders this is usually expressed in the leadership of a team of teachers responsible for a subject or phase of education.

Subject leaders work at the pivotal point of the interaction of principle and practice, translating the values of the school into the consistent, concrete experience of every pupil and adult. If school leadership is about 'doing the right things' then middle leadership is about 'doing things right' in the context of the right things for the team. This requires bridging the strategic and the operational; in essence, relating the school to the classroom, and vice versa, in a way which ensures that policy is grounded in the realities of the school and that middle leaders have the resources to implement the policies at a classroom level.

A credible, evidence based definition of the characteristics of effective teaching must be central to any characterisation of subject leadership. The Sutton Trust report *What Makes Great Teaching?* (Coe et al., 2014: 2–3) provides a very clear and authoritative view as to the key priorities of school leadership and subject leaders, in particular:

1 *(Pedagogical) content knowledge (Strong evidence of impact on student outcomes)*

   The most effective teachers have deep knowledge of the subjects they teach [...] [T]eachers must also understand the ways students think about the content, be able to evaluate the thinking behind students' own methods, and identify students' common misconceptions.

2 *Quality of instruction (Strong evidence of impact on student outcomes)*

   Includes elements such as effective questioning and use of assessment by teachers. Specific practices, like reviewing previous learning, providing model responses for students, giving adequate time for practice to embed skills securely and progressively introducing new learning (scaffolding) are also elements of high quality instruction.

On the basis of linking the main elements of effective middle leadership with what the evidence suggests about the core components of great teaching, it is possible to identify the key elements of subject leadership. These might be defined as follows:

→ Having a well-articulated, ambitious vision based on high expectations for all pupils and an excellent understanding of current developments and thinking in the subject.

→ Personal credibility in terms of effective pedagogy, subject knowledge and the design of teaching and learning resources and strategies.

→ Challenging poor performance and securing consistency across the team by eliminating variation but celebrating variety (i.e. a balance of control and trust).

→ Modelling best practice through collaborative working and by challenging colleagues to innovate and develop new approaches.

→ Effective monitoring, self-evaluation and action planning clearly focused on securing consistency, supporting improvement and diagnosing support strategies.

→ Consistent use of data about pupils' performance as the basis for targeted interventions, focusing on the most disadvantaged and the most able, as appropriate.

→ Provision of relevant professional learning and development centred on coaching and classroom focused action research in order to foster and share best practice.

→ Efficient and effective use of resources to support excellent teaching and learning.

→ Working with peers and providing leadership to secure whole school approaches to the drive for improvement.

→ Working collaboratively with other teams in the school and teams from other schools.

Ask your subject heads to carry out a self-review against these areas using resource 3A(i). Then use resource 3A(ii) to collate these results into a single document highlighting main strengths and weaknesses. Resource 3A(iii) can be used to plan action/support to improve performance across all leaders.

Key questions

How would you assess the current level of shared understanding of effective teaching and learning across your school and your team?

What shared model of learning informs your team's professional practice?

What evidence do you have to corroborate your view of your team's focus on consistent, high quality teaching and learning?

What documentation is available to support your team's shared understanding of teaching and learning?

In your role as a middle leader, what proportion of your time do you spend working with colleagues on shared approaches to teaching and learning?

Resources (Download)

3A(i)   Self-review sheet for subject leaders

3A(ii)   Collating the results from subject leaders

3A(iii)   Actions to improve subject leadership

3B

**B   Cross-curricular roles –
leading strands outside the subject area**

Why is this an important topic for conversation?

In a rapidly changing world the demands on education increase every year. It is no longer appropriate for schools to simply serve as conduits for delivering subject knowledge to pupils. Increasingly, society expects its schools to address a whole range of wider issues. The list, which seems to lengthen on a monthly basis, covers an eye-watering range including health, mental health, sex and relationships, morality, citizenship, multiculturalism, the environment, community engagement/safety, cyber safety, entrepreneurship, and careers. Add to this the new cross-school tasks related to teaching and learning and we have an explanation for the huge rise in the number of non-subject specific roles appearing in both primary and secondary schools.

Key quotes for the section

> Who is responsible for developing approaches to cross-curricular teaching and learning? Is it the responsibility of the whole school through the implementation of a whole school policy or strategy? Or is it the responsibility of individual subject leaders and their relationships with other teachers or wider local networks?
>
> **(Savage, 2010: 16)**

> Education is not preparation for life; education is life itself.
>
> **(Dewey, 1938: 239)**

> Education is what remains after one has forgotten what one has learned in school.
>
> **(Anon.)**

> The aim of education should be to teach us how to think, rather than what to think. To improve our minds, so as to enable us to think for ourselves, rather than to load the memory with thoughts of other men.
>
> **(attributed to Bill Beattie)**

> Teaching kids to count is fine, but teaching them what counts is best.
>
> **(attributed to Bob Talbert)**

Section discussion

Opinions on the purpose of education are varied, as can be seen from the quotes above. Very few people would assert that the only purpose of education is to replicate the knowledge of the last generation (although many governments act as if it is). Many believe that the key role of education is to prepare young people for adult life, the nature of which is rarely limited to subject areas. So, if our schools are to be more than fact givers, shouldn't these 'extra dimensions' be organised and not just left to chance? Clearly a rhetorical question, but if these issues are so important for young people then their delivery must be organised.

The follow-up question is set out in the quote from Savage: 'Who is responsible?' The official answer is probably 'the head teacher', who, after all, is legally responsible for anything that goes on in the building and its environs. However, given that most head teachers are not short of things to do, this may not be the best way to progress such important work. Many school leaders describe their work as akin to keeping all the plates spinning as in a circus act; adding another plate to spin is not likely to produce the required development. This realisation has led to a tendency to allocate cross-curricular roles to members of staff without a current major leadership role. Sometimes this is simply because 'it will be good for your career'; in other cases, it has small financial and/or timetabling benefits (e.g. it fills up a few periods of unallocated time!).

This trend means that key development areas are given to less experienced members of staff – individuals who have less familiarity with implementing change and potentially have less standing with the teachers they are trying to lead. An added complication is that much of the teaching profession has developed around the central concept of imparting subject knowledge, and therefore can view tasks outside their 'core role' as being less important. The result of these combined forces is that many of these cross-curricular roles are not as effective as they need to be and can be a source of frustration to the post-holder. Where roles like this are successful they are almost always held by a very high energy individual.

So, if you are considering giving leadership responsibility for a strategic topic to someone else, there are some important conversations to have. Use resource 3B(i) to investigate if allocating the role to a particular individual is really the best route. Write the cross-curricular area you are wanting to improve in the central star, then consider each question, looking at how you currently lead that area and identifying the reasons for delegating the additional responsibilities. If the exercise produces clear evidence for the creation of a new role, ensure the whole team takes responsibility for the support that you have identified on the resource.

If the decision has already been made and responsibility has been given to an individual to lead a cross-curricular theme across the school, then it is vital that this person has a direct link with the entire school leadership team. Without a clear line of support, any non-subject specific role will inevitably be considered as 'additional'. It is vital that the value of this area is given prominence in every task connected to it. Resource 3B(ii) should be completed by the person with responsibility for the area.

To avoid any tasks being resigned to the 'might get around to it in a moment – if I have one' pile, it is important to identify why the cross-curricular work is so essential. In any school there are competing demands on time: teachers are expected to plan and mark their work, provide pastoral development and communicate with parents as a standard part of their job. Your new additional task may be of vital importance to you, but do not assume it has the same significance for all your colleagues. One way to prepare for this is to consider the negative side of any task you wish them to undertake. Fill in resource 3B(iii) from a negative perspective – why might someone *not* complete this task? Once you have identified reasons why the work may not be as well received as you would like, share these across the leadership team. Identify ways that you can all support the development. If you are unable to find the time (or reasons) to support the initiative, you may need to ask yourselves why you are doing it.

If you remain convinced of the vital nature of the proposed cross-curricular work, it is a useful strategy to plan small ways to keep the topic alive in the staffroom. Use the grid in resource 3B(iv) to record your plans for the next half term. Ensure that most of the ideas are not time consuming and are easy to implement. They might include a brief spot in staff briefings (or even during a lunch meeting with pizza), emails or posters.

Whatever you do, make sure the focus is on why this is so important for the pupils. Remember, if it isn't important, you shouldn't be wasting staff time on it!

Key questions

Why is the cross-curricular area of importance to the pupils?

What is wrong with continuing as you are?

Is giving leadership to an individual the best way of moving this on?

How will this new work be perceived by staff?

How can the initiative be supported?

Resources (Download)

3B(i)	Thinking about delegating responsibility
3B(ii)	Developing the planning for the delivery of a cross-curricular area
3B(iii)	Investigating the negative aspects of a proposed task
3B(iv)	Reinforcing the importance of a development

3C

C   Pastoral roles – looking after the human side

Why is this an important topic for conversation?

News headlines keep proclaiming that the number of young people with mental health issues is increasing every year. Other reports highlight rising levels of socio-economic disadvantage among local communities. Add to this deepening global and environmental concerns, and we have a challenging backdrop to the development of young people. Once the whole societal soup becomes agitated by new instant ways to pass information and insults, we have a toxic setting for many school communities. More than ever before, schools need strong teams of staff to support pupils' welfare; naturally, these teams need great leaders to coordinate the work they do.

Key quotes for the section

> Unfortunately, many young people experience such intense and sustained changes to and violations of their core sense of self that they are unable to engage with the process of maturation. Their interactions with significant others, usually people in authority, have involved the intentional or unintentional misuse or abuse of personal power.
>
> **(Harris, 2007: 4)**

> Just asking a child to put something away, or to promise not to wear a banned item again, is not really a good idea. If they promise to put the hat away for the rest of the day, they might. Then again, they may wear it into the next lesson and tell the teacher that the previous teacher had allowed them to do so. The second teacher then becomes resentful of the first teacher and, in that case, decides they won't confiscate the hat either. Poor old teacher number three does what she is supposed to and asks for the hat. To the student she now seems unreasonable. In a sense, she is. The hypocrisy of her colleagues has undermined her and the school's values and left her in a far more difficult situation. It's all about consistency. You're swimming against the tide without it.
>
> **(Rowe, 2013: 11)**

> Discipline is not what you do to yourself or what anyone else does to you. It's what you do for yourself.
>
> (Roberson, 2012: 16)

Section discussion

As outlined in the introduction to this section, and very eloquently emphasised in the quote from Belinda Harris, the world is a challenging place in which to be developing into an adult. When these increased pressures coincide with an increased focus on the level of achievement gained, it can be no surprise that the need for quality pastoral support is growing every year.

In the early days of schooling, the class teacher was expected to be responsible for every aspect of a child's education (i.e. teaching and learning). As specialisation increased and the demands of examination systems became more complex, many schools felt the need to employ extra staff to help provide support outside the tight confines of subject learning. The increasing prevalence of mental health problems, combined with a decrease in the amount of specialised provision available, has resulted in a large increase in the number of staff employed with at least some pastoral responsibility.

As financial pressures squeeze school budgets, it is inevitable that some schools will review the amount of money they spend on non-teaching roles. It may be an activity you wish to undertake for your own school. Resource 3C(i) provides a simple, graphic way to collect your thinking. What is your initial opinion of the balance of expenditure between the pastoral and academic sides? If you had to reduce spending in your school, on which side of the scale would the budget cut have the least detriment to pupil progress? The answer may vary from school to school, but it may be that successful pastoral roles are having a greater effect than those which purely deliver in the academic arena. The link between academic achievement and deprivation is well documented, so the potential for pastoral roles to have a major impact in reducing negative effects should not be a surprise.

Any pressure to reduce the amount of spending on pastoral support increases the requirement for quality leadership in this area. A clear understanding of the function of any pastoral support is an essential first step. Without clarity there is real danger that impossible expectations become the norm.

What is the core reason for a particular pastoral role? What problem is it supposed to solve? In what ways do you need all staff to play their part in addressing this issue?

Use resource 3C(ii) to analyse the demands being placed on the role. Identify all the issues you want the role to address and write them in the left hand column. Try to avoid vague, generic headings such as 'achievement' or 'behaviour' as these decrease the chance of ever fulfilling the demands (e.g. what is 'good behaviour'?). Instead, identify specific areas you hope to improve. For each of the identified requirements, consider how the role could bring this about, how likely it is to solve the problem on its own and what extra support is required.

In some ways, pastoral roles that are focused on supporting the educational development of a particular learning disability are easier to manage: the child (or group of children) have a special need that can be met by 'expert' support. The classroom teacher looks to the 'expert' to help not only the pupils directly but also to help build the learning relationship between the pupil and the teacher. In this case, all expectations are being met, the role is a fulfilling one and it provides benefits to both pupils and teacher.

However, many pastoral roles are created with general aims related to behaviour management. Leading in this area is much more fraught with difficulty. If a school identifies that it is concerned about behaviour getting in the way of quality learning in the classroom, simply expecting one individual to 'solve' this is unrealistic and has every chance of being counterproductive. If a classroom teacher is led to believe that any poor behaviour by pupils in their care will be resolved by another staff member can lead to an abdication of responsibility or even the belief that the power to address the issue is not within their own skill set.

As indicated by the quote from Jeremy Rowe, the key weapon in the battle to improve behaviour is the consistency of approach from staff in the school. Therefore, a leader with responsibility in this area would be advised to focus much of their effort on producing consistency across the staff. Resource 3C(iii) offers a method to identify the behaviour that the school wishes to tackle and the staff behaviours that need to be uniformly applied. For example, if shouting out in class is the issue to be addressed, the expected response by teachers should be identified in the chart. Each teacher uses the resource to note their successes and issues in this area. These 'difficulties with compliance' should then be used to improve staff training or amend the guidance. Spending pastoral time in this way is likely to be more successful than firefighting the consequences of inconsistency.

Pastoral leaders will always find themselves in the middle of a dilemma – on one hand understanding why a child is acting in a particular way, and on the other not wanting to allow the child to accept that this is their only option. As the Jim Roberson quote suggests, a pastoral leader is most effective when they are helping pupils take responsibility for their own behaviour, rather than trying to stamp the school's expectations of behaviour on to the child.

Key questions

Is the pastoral system in your school sufficiently valued?

What do you want the pastoral system to achieve?

Can the pastoral system realistically achieve this?

How can the pastoral system help classroom teachers to be more effective?

What does the school mean by 'good behaviour'?

Resources (Download)

3C(i)   Judging the balance in expenditure between academic and pastoral support

3C(ii)   Investigating the requirements of a pastoral role

3C(iii) Creating a consistent approach towards pupil behaviour

3D

D   A question of balance

Why is this an important topic for conversation?

Middle leaders are literally in the middle. On the one hand they derive their authority and responsibilities from senior leaders and are accountable to them; on the other hand they are working on a daily basis with their team, holding them to account but also securing their day-to-day engagement and commitment. It is this balance of the formal and informal that is essential to effective leadership, but it does require a repertoire of skills and strategies.

Key quotes for the section

> Allegiance in uplifting organizations is not about deference to those of higher rank. Nor is it about mutual back-scratching – that is, exchanging services in return for past favors or future rewards. Rather, loyalty or allegiance is about committing to people and caring for their lives.
>
> **(Hargreaves et al., 2014: 94)**

> Before you are a leader, success is all about growing yourself. When you become a leader, success is all about growing others.
>
> **(Jack Welch, quoted in Lowe, 2007: 88)**

> Keep your fears to yourself, but share your courage with others.
>
> **(Anon.)**

Section discussion

All schools are to some extent hierarchical; indeed, our education system seems to function on hierarchies. For example, given what we know about the importance of early years provision in cognitive and social development, it is evident that it should be funded at a level that recognises its relative impact – any money spent at this stage can save much more later on. School hierarchies vary enormously in terms of their rigour and formality. It is very difficult to imagine a formal hierarchy working in a special school or early years setting. It is very much a matter of national culture and historical expectations.

In Finland, school leaders belong to the same trade union as teachers, and all leaders have a teaching commitment: 'Leaders do not see themselves as "the boss" – nor are they perceived as such by the teachers. Relationships are not very hierarchical, and in schools it is often difficult to distinguish teachers from support staff' (Hargreaves et al., 2008: 83). This perspective is reinforced by Sahlberg (2015: 127): 'Teachers rely on their leaders' vision and the principal understands and trusts teachers' work. Therefore leadership and management in Finnish schools are informal but effective.'

However, in Britain it seems to be the case that the older the student and the larger the institution, the more formal the relationships. Given the importance of the role of middle leaders, as discussed in section 3A, it is important to explore how middle leaders work in this potentially complex situation of being 'in the middle' of the school hierarchy – both being held to account while also holding others to account. The tension can become really significant when subject team members hold senior positions in the school hierarchy.

Successful middle leaders learn to work through a range of complex interacting variables and find a way forward by reconciling a number of potentially competing imperatives:

Control	Trust
Power	Influence
Status	Moral authority
Formal relationships	Informal relationships
Tight controls	Loose understandings
Performativity based accountability	Professional accountability
Compliance	Engagement
Top down	Bottom up

Analyse the performance of the middle leaders and leadership team using resource 3D(i). Is there a consistency of approach? If not, why not? If so, are you happy with the consensus?

There is a myth that high performance is more likely to be achieved through the factors on the left hand side of the table on page 63; hence the focus on performativity, quantifiable outcomes and narrowly reductionist and instrumental definitions of performance. However:

> *Countless sources tell us that sustained high performance comes from focusing more on values than profits. Great companies encourage exceptional performance when they inspire a driving passion for the work that their people do. Enduring success occurs when we feel that our work is creating emotional and social value.* (Hargreaves et al., 2014: 5)

One of the pivotal challenges facing middle leaders is that they have to work within a context over which they have limited control. We know that the modelling of behaviour and the use of language by senior leaders are two of the most significant influences on school culture and the nature of working relationships. Middle leaders can therefore find themselves in the situation where the prevailing culture in the school actually goes against what they believe to be appropriate working relationships. There may, of course, be very good reasons for this – for example, a school that is in crisis by virtue of sustained poor performance may well need a period of relatively draconian leadership; however, this is unsustainable over the long term. The movement from the left hand side of the table to the right is fundamental in terms of developing leadership capacity and sustainability.

It is important to stress that, in spite of all of the pressures towards conformity, top down policies and imposed criteria for success, schools remain very different. It is both inspiring and worrying that schools working in similar contexts are so different; nevertheless, it does indicate that there is scope for middle leaders to work within national and school policies but to do so in a way that is both moral and professional.

In order to navigate an apposite path in relation to the aforementioned table, middle leaders need to explore and develop a range of skills and strategies in order to respond appropriately and effectively to the demands of school policy, as well as the legitimate expectations and needs of their team. Such skills and strategies might include:

→ High levels of intrapersonal intelligence; in particular, the ability to understand the way that others perceive us and our emotional response to those perceptions.

→ A rich repertoire of strategies related to interpersonal literacy – in broad terms, sophisticated, empathic responses expressed in listening and understanding, sensitivity to alternative perspectives and recognition of potentially conflicting values.

→ The ability to communicate complex ideas and issues in a way that is engaging, compelling and persuasive.

→ Demonstrating respect and recognition of the imperatives informing colleagues' stances, but being willing and able to challenge through appropriate questioning.

→ Working through kindness, respect and courtesy in order to create a culture that optimises engagement and commitment and models the relationships needed for deep learning.

→ Building trust by allowing others to lead aspects of the school, providing real and significant choices and encouraging experimentation and innovation.

Encourage self-analysis and coaching among the middle leaders. Give resource 3D(ii) to your middle leaders and ask them to review themselves against the skills listed above. There is space for peer monitoring, if required, and questions to help the leader identify the skills they would like to develop further.

Of course, there has to be formal accountability through performance management, but this can be a positive experience if the bureaucratic element is minimised and the principles set out above are used. This means middle leaders are working in a professionally respectful and mature way, which is a reflection of how they, in turn, are treated.

Key questions

How would you characterise the prevailing relationships in your school in terms of senior and middle leaders and middle leaders and their teams?

Are you personally comfortable with the notion of 'working through kindness, respect and courtesy'? What might that look like in practice?

To what extent are senior leaders modelling appropriate behaviours for middle leaders?

Is there consistency across the middle leaders in the school in terms of what they do and how they do it?

What support and training is available for middle leaders in the relational aspects of their work?

Resources (Download)

3D(i)   Analysing middle leadership in the school
3D(ii)   Self-analysis/coaching support for middle leaders

E   Working in teams

Why is this an important topic for conversation?

As discussed in earlier parts of this section, the role of the middle leader can be one of the most challenging in a school. Middle leaders often find themselves in a tricky position, frequently dividing leadership responsibility with a heavy teaching commitment, and sometimes feeling they are in a no man's land between the leaders and the teachers. This can be a very lonely place, being neither one of the teaching staff nor one of the leaders. One way to combat this isolation is to develop the teams with whom middle leaders work – both the teams for whom they have responsibility and the team of other middle leaders in the school.

Key quotes for the section

> Remember, teamwork begins by building trust. And the only way to do that is to overcome our need for invulnerability.
>
> **(Lencioni, 2002: 63)**

> The strength of the team is each individual member. The strength of each member is the team.
>
> **(attributed to Phil Jackson)**

> Collaboration allows teachers to capture each other's fund of collective intelligence.
>
> **(Schmoker, 1999: 100)**

> Unity is strength ... when there is teamwork and collaboration, wonderful things can be achieved.
>
> **(Mattie Stepanek, quoted in Flinders et al., 2013: vi)**

3E

> The greater the loyalty of a group toward the group, the greater is the motivation among the members to achieve the goals of the group, and the greater the probability that the group will achieve its goals.
>
> **(Rensis Likert, quoted in O'Rourke and Yarbrough, 2008: 35)**

> [W]hat principles should apply to working relationships among school staff? Does a defensible approach to school leadership imply shared leadership and, if so, which aspects of leadership should be shared, by whom, with whom, how equally, and under what circumstances?
>
> **(Wallace, 2001: 153)**

Section discussion

The collection of short quotes above is a small selection from the plethora of those available from schools, business and sport celebrating the power of working in teams. The fact that an effective team possesses a power greater than the individual contribution of each team member is rarely challenged. For middle leaders, the unique pressures outlined in the introduction to this section highlight the need for them to maximise the support from their teams – both their subject team and the school's team of middle leaders.

The area team

For subject leaders in secondary schools, this team will be those teachers who work in the area of their responsibility, while for primary subject leads it may consist of a group of teachers across the whole school. For pastoral leaders or those with responsibilities for whole school topics, the team in question may be the complete staff team. This quickly highlights a key fact: teachers are often members of more than one team, therefore the middle leader is automatically in competition for teachers' commitment and focus. As outlined in the first chapter of *Leadership Dialogues* (2014), the whole school leader is at their most effective when there is clarity in values and ethos across the school. This is equally true in the middle leader's team. However, if the middle leader attempts to develop an ethos at odds with that of the whole school, then this would obviously serve to undermine the stability of the whole organisation.

The first step for the middle leader is (a) to ensure that they fully understand what is expected of their team, and then (b) to define the staff ethos and attitude needed to deliver these expectations. Armed with this information, the plan for action for the department team should be expressed as clearly and positively as possible. Resource 3E(i) provides a suitable form on which to start planning. By positioning the whole school ethos alongside area planning from the earliest stages, it is more likely that the work will fit with other priorities in the school. If a middle leader allows the work in their area to be simply driven by themselves at a personal level, not only will it be extremely heavy on their time but it is also less likely to be successful. Therefore, the focus should be to encourage whole team responsibility for the action. If the plan matches the whole school ethos then the team can concentrate on how delivering this also achieves the whole school goals. In other words, these actions are not additional but are core to the happy completion of their role within the school.

If the area of responsibility is whole school, then this strategy is even more important. Cross-curricular responsibilities are too easily dismissed by staff as supplementary to their core work, especially if they are seen as the 'pet topic' of an individual. If, as a middle leader, you are concerned that your area of responsibility is not progressing as quickly as you would like, then looking at how the staff prioritise your area could be quite useful. Resource 3E(ii) offers a format to investigate the issue with your team. Tailor the form to suit your needs, identifying the area you want to consider and any other particular priorities in your school.

The team of middle leaders

Clearly, creating cohesion within their own team should be a major priority for the middle leader, but a number of the barriers and complications they meet in their role can be improved by developing a strong horizontal team across all the middle leaders within the school. As discussed earlier, it is normal for those in the role to feel isolated, with many teachers not fully appreciating the tensions placed on those in middle leadership roles. To work closely with others who are experiencing the same attitudes can provide genuine support.

If there isn't already an existing mechanism within the school for middle leaders to meet together, then work with the senior leaders to instigate one. The series of questions posed in Mike Wallace's quote is a good place to start. When the group meet, resource 3E(iii) is a good way to collect information to help pull the work of the middle leadership team together. It is a good way to increase the understanding between middle leaders about their common issues. This increased understanding should result in a decrease in inter-area conflict and an increase in the coming together of middle leaders to consider projects which meet more than their own targets. As we have already highlighted, the more a school has a cohesive ethos, the greater its likelihood of success; and the more that middle leaders understand the effect of their own team on school values, the more feasible it is that the school will be a cohesive unit.

Another productive area for the middle leader team is to work on improving levels of trust within the school, particularly considering areas where trust is lower than expected. By addressing any issues found, involving as wide a group as possible, levels of trust in the school can be rebuilt. As a result, cross-curricular work will be more successful in this new climate.

Key questions

How do you make your area of responsibility important to others?

How does your area fit into the whole school ethos?

How can you make your area not 'all about you'?

Do you share your plans with other middle leaders?

How could others help you in your work?

Resources (Download)

3E(i)	Planning the work of the area team
3E(ii)	Investigating your work priorities
3E(iii)	Improving middle leader team cohesion

Managing resources

A   Making better use of your time

Why is this an important topic for conversation?

It is unlikely that any school leader needs to ask why this topic is urgent. Demands on schools increase every year, and the expectations for school leaders multiply with them. Looked at from any angle, making more effective use of a leader's time must be a priority. Viewed from a purely business perspective, leaders are often the most expensive resource in the school and therefore to not have them operating at their most efficient would be undesirable. Viewed from a purely human perspective, a stressed leader who does not feel able to support their colleagues is also to be avoided.

Key quotes for the section

> One thing is for certain: in order to find the time to fulfil your current management obligations and still become a better leader, you must change. Sometimes you must change what you do, which means saying 'No' to work that might be comfortable but is simply not valuable enough to keep doing.
>
> **(Coats, n.d.)**

> As I read through the various tips [on time management], I realized that our obsession with managing our calendars has actually resulted in our calendars managing us. I realized that my perspective that I am time-starved is actually stopping me from being effective as a leader.
>
> **(Inman, 2013)**

4A

> The key is not to prioritize what's on your schedule, but to schedule your priorities.
>
> **(Covey, 2004: 161)**

> Time is what we want most, but what, alas! we use worst.
>
> **(Penn, 1903 [1682]: xxviii)**

Section discussion

The first two quotes above are representative of the plethora of advice to be found on the Internet. You will not be surprised to learn that there is little consensus – there is no simple answer that will suddenly transform your working (or personal) life. You will find some 'experts' who will tell you that you need a special system to help you control your time, while others will tell you that that is the last thing you should do. What is clear is that any successful technique is dependent on the personality of the individual and the context in which they work. However, there are some simple principles that can be adapted to suit most leaders, all of which require you to understand exactly what you want to achieve and if it is possible.

School leaders will often complain that they are stressed by the lack of time. This is an interesting phenomenon; clearly we all share the same space–time continuum (with the exception of any readers who are currently travelling in a rocket!) and the length of the day is the same for all of us. So, it is not about having enough time but about having control over how we make use of that time. We feel pressure when we realise that the things we are expected to do more than fill the hours we have available to do them. In other words, the heart of the problem lies in our expectations (or the expectations of those around us). If we are working towards achieving the impossible, then it should come as no surprise when we don't achieve it.

One of the first steps to gaining control over your workload is to carry out an in/out review of the demands you are placing on yourself. Use resource 4A(i) to analyse the tasks you need to do in the next week. The form requires you to identify every task for the week ahead, outline the expected time you need to allocate to it and the importance you associate with the task (1 = high importance, 5 = low importance). The resource will help you to prioritise the allocation of time relative to the significance of each activity. Hopefully the figures will be closer to 1 than 5. If not, the implication is that you are allocating too much of your time to unimportant tasks. This may be because the person influencing your tasks does not place the same value on some of them as you do. It is vital that this is addressed at this point of the analysis, as you should not be worrying about managing your time to complete tasks of little value.

Assuming your tasks are more significant ones, the next part of your analysis is to see how much time you have available for the work. Use resource 4A(ii) to identify the unallocated time you have in a typical week. It is imperative that you approach this task with a desire to find out the truth, rather than for any alternative motive – honesty is the key. Try to spot any period of time that you could use in another way – for example, if you have meetings that could be dropped, free up the time available and add the meeting to the tasks you have identified in resource 4A(i) as being of low importance.

Once you have completed both of these forms, compare the hours you need for critical tasks with the time you have available. If the two are similar, then monitor the reality using the original form you completed – was your time allocation accurate? Identify any items that were more time heavy than you predicted. Ascertain any tasks that are taking up excessive amounts of your time but are relatively trivial. Is your hourly importance rating higher or lower than you predicted? As a leadership team, compare these figures honestly and consider the implication on the leadership of the school. Look for practical ways to shift the actual hourly importance rating for the whole leadership team. As a general rule, doing things that are urgent but not essential is not the road to success.

Many leaders recognise the scenario in which they have so much to do that it seems almost impossible. This to-do mountain has the ability to completely paralyse otherwise rational human beings. The gift of an unexpected additional 15 minutes, rather than being a source of relief, can sometimes become a further pressure, with the stressed leader actually doing nothing ('It isn't long enough to make an impact on such a mountain!') and at the end of the 15 minutes they now add guilt to their growing list of anxieties. While to-do lists are not everyone's cup of tea (as demonstrated in Henna Inman's quote) many leaders find some basic organisational tools a release from continually holding the action list in their head.

Resource 4A(iii) is a useful tool if you suffer from the 'How do I make better use of a short gap?' syndrome. Print the table and keep it near to hand. As any new task is given to you (or emerges from the ether, as is often the case), quickly decide how long it will take to complete, rank its importance (from 1–5) and add it to the appropriate column in the table. This will take under a minute but can be at the heart of a different attitude towards using your time well. If a meeting finishes early and you gain five minutes, rather than impersonate a rabbit in the headlights of a car, choose the most important item from the appropriate column, get the task done and strike a line through it as you complete it. The effect of completing a task (even though it is just one of the smaller jobs) helps to create a more positive mixture of brain chemicals, which in turn contributes to your overall sense of well-being.

While the majority of this section is about your own relationship – the tasks you have to complete and the time you have to complete them – it is vital that the issue of effective time management is regarded as a whole team issue rather than just an individual one. Effective teams help to reduce time pressures across the whole team, not just for each individual.

Key questions

Do you have too much work for your available time?

Are you stressed by the mismatch between the two?

Are any of your tasks urgent but not important?

If so, why are you doing them?

Could you make more use of the little bits of time you have?

Resources (Download)

4A(i)	Analysing the tasks to be completed
4A(ii)	Identifying available time
4A(iii)	What shall I do now? – a collection of time appropriate tasks to fill a gap

B   Meetings that work

Why is this an important topic for conversation?

With leadership time at a premium it is completely nonsensical for a group to focus a large proportion of their collective time sitting around a table in fruitless activity. No one ever sets out to let this happen but most people will recall many occasions when it has. Therefore, developing some simple attitudes and practices which will improve the effectiveness of meetings has to be worthy of consideration.

Key quotes for the section

> We are a meeting society – a world made up of small groups that come together to share information, plan, solve problems, criticise or praise, make new decisions or find out what went wrong with old ones. Governments, businesses, schools, clubs, families – all are built up from groups of men, women and children. Regardless of their values or goals, individual members of these groups must get together in order to function. When three or more people work together face to face we call this a 'meeting'.
>
> **(Doyle and Straus, 1993: 3)**

> Meetings are windows on the soul of business: they reveal the quality of its management. Well-organized, well-conducted meetings bespeak an effective organization. Meetings afflicted with sloppy planning, flimsy agendas, and fuzzy expectations indicate a not-so-effective one.
>
> **(Carney, 2008)**

> If you had to identify, in one word, the reason why the human race has not achieved and never will achieve its full potential, that word would be meetings.
>
> **(attributed to Dave Barry)**

Section discussion

Numerous books are published across the world aimed at helping businesses to run efficient meetings. All identify the lost revenue to organisations caused by poorly run meetings. One could argue that the issue is even more urgent in the world of education, where participants are in the classroom for the majority of their day, and therefore try to make the maximum use of every 'spare' moment. A wasted 90 minutes in education is even more frustrating if it represents most of the available non-teaching time a school leader has in a week.

Use resource 4B(i) to analyse the available leadership time you have available within your school. By using this tool (which guides you towards finding out how much time each leader can reasonably be expected to contribute to leadership), you will acquire a rough idea of the number of leadership hours the school has the potential to use each week. The amount of (or lack of) time arrived at is often a surprise to the SLT. It is normal to have high expectations for leaders – after all, we have shown how valuable their contribution is in almost every aspect of school life. However, sometimes these aims can lose sight of the limited size of the available resource. For some schools, a 90 minute leadership team meeting can drain a significant proportion of the leadership time available for that week. (Count the number of minutes and multiply it by the number of attendees to measure the leadership commitment of your school.) Did the effect of your last meeting have a greater effect on the development of your school than the separate contributions that all the individuals would have made if left to their own devices? If the answer is no, then you need to do something about it – and fast!

A good first step towards improving the quality of the leadership meetings in your school is to have an honest look at the effectiveness of the last two you have attended. Ideally, do this analysis as a whole group, ensuring that the meeting convenor is at the heart of this (otherwise it may feel like a criticism of that individual). Resource 4B(ii) should be completed by as many attendees as possible, each using the minutes of the meeting as a prompt. If possible, share people's different views of the effectiveness of the meeting because one person's 'wonderful sounding board' might be another's 'complete waste of time'. Have an open discussion across the team about how the arrangements for meetings could be improved to make more effective use of everyone's time.

It is better if the group agrees its own rules for meetings, as individuals are more likely to adhere to a new format and set of procedures if they have introduced them. However, here a few examples of good practice that you might want to steer the group towards:

→ An agenda with items contributed from as wide a cross-section of the group as possible.

→ Each item to have an allocated (and realistic) time slot on the agenda.

→ The agenda to be constructed from available topics (rather than simply the first eight things anyone thinks of!). If the agenda is too full, don't just cross your fingers and hope – decide what is most important to be discussed and arrange the agenda to suit. Even though it might constitute an extra meeting, a small sub-group looking critically over the agenda before it is circulated can actually make the group more efficient.

→ Circulate the agenda at least two working days in advance, ensuring that everyone who is expected to lead the discussion on a particular item is fully prepared to do so. Encourage dialogue about the agenda: are the right things on it? Have you missed anything?

→ Make sure the start time is realistic. Nothing is more likely to lead to an ineffective meeting than one with a tight agenda which starts 15 minutes late. School leaders, particularly those with a pastoral responsibility, find it very difficult to achieve a start time just 15 minutes after the end of the school day. Set the start time together and then commit to everyone achieving it. Look into using support staff to ensure that leaders are able to meet at the agreed time.

→ Ensure the temperature of the room is conducive to active engagement (a study from Helsinki University would suggest 20–22°C – see Seppänen et al., 2004).

→ Have refreshments available at least 15 minutes before the due start time. If possible, include some treats (they can always be healthy treats if you wish!). Again, a little effort to make the setting of the room pleasant can make those at the meeting feel they are valued, which will produce results far greater than the effort put in.

→ Start your meeting by looking at the agenda and agreeing what you all want to achieve in the session. Ensure the timings are followed precisely. Agree that any item which overruns will be terminated at that point and continued in another way – either by email or by inclusion in a future agenda.

→ If time allows, include a round of 30 second 'positives' – each person saying one thing they are very happy about that week.

→ Ask if anyone has any burning issues that they want to raise during the 'any other business' (AOB) slot – make a quick decision on whether they will be permitted and ensure these do not take more than the allocated time. Some items may have to be left for another meeting or a different approach. Trying to force too much into the time available is always counterproductive.

→ At the end of each item (or when the allotted time is up) conclude the item with agreed actions – these are the only things that need to be recorded in the minutes (a possible format is included as resource 4B(iii)).

→ Finish the meeting in a controlled and positive way – if possible, highlight what the achievement of the meeting will be.

Meetings are a self-fulfilling prophecy: if those attending expect it to be a waste of time, it probably will be. If the group develops its own routines and ambitions, the positive attitudes going into the meeting will be amplified in a positive feedback loop. No one minds meetings if they feel they are a valuable use of their time.

Key questions

Do we know how much leadership time the school has available?

How valuable are the current leadership team meetings?

How could they be improved?

How many of the above actions could become common practice for your group?

Resources (Download)

4B(i)	Calculating the leadership hours available for your school
4B(ii)	Investigating the effectiveness of your meetings
4B(iii)	A possible structure for recording the minutes of a meeting

C   After the meeting – ensuring impact

Why is this an important topic for conversation?

In many ways meetings are the last refuge of amateurism in education management. While a wide repertoire of skills is now recognised as essential to effective leadership, all too often meetings in schools are less than effective. It is assumed that educated professionals are in some way naturally proficient in coming together to make decisions. Equally, there is often a reluctance to give away authority because of a perceived need to retain control and to micromanage.

Key quotes for the section

> Meetings are of critical importance in co-ordinating effort and effecting change, and a very important part of the manager's role is to ensure that they are vehicles for communication and action rather than for confusion and frustration. This will be achieved by 'helicoptering' above the hurly-burly of the discussion, asking what we wish to achieve, being aware of the behavioural processes at work and trying to structure the meeting in such a way as to channel positively the energies of those involved.
>
> **(Everard and Morris, 1996: 52)**

> KPIs (key performance indicators) can often help team members to attain high performance; however, when they feel under excess pressure to meet these KPIs in situations where goals are unclear or the consequences of failing are punitive, people typically adopt self-defeating practices driven by fear of failure rather than ambitions for success. [...] In education [this] leads to narrowing the curriculum and preparing children for tests, rather than actually teaching them *how to learn*.
>
> **(Hargreaves et al., 2014: 8; original emphasis)**

Section discussion

Meetings are essential to any model of organisational effectiveness. From strategic policy making to routine administration they are the basis for translating principle into practice. As such, what happens *after* the meeting is at least as important as any discussion that takes place during the meeting. In fact, it could be argued that a crucial test of the effectiveness of a team or meeting is its ability to convert values and aspirations into concrete experiences.

The key to ensuring impact seems to be encapsulated in the question, 'Who does what, when?' This simple formulation can be broken down into its specific components, but it is crucial that the 'how' is left to the team to decide.

Who refers to the individual (or group) who has the delegated responsibility for ensuring that the desired outcome is achieved. In practical terms this means:

→ Who has the authority to ensure that the outcome is achieved?

→ Who is accountable for the quality of the outcome?

→ Do those involved have the right blend of knowledge and skills?

→ What time and resources do they require?

What is probably best reviewed in a reworking of the classic formulation of SMART targets. Intended outcomes should be agreed upon with due consideration for:

→ *Specificity*: clearly defined with no ambiguity and clear areas of discretion and compliance.

→ *Measurability*: where appropriate, defined in terms of specific outcomes and quality criteria.

→ *Appropriateness*: fit for purpose in the context of the school and possible within appropriate resources.

→ *Research*: drawing on valid and reliable evidence to inform choices and actions.

→ *Training*: support and development provided as necessary.

When is perhaps the most significant element as schools almost invariably perceive themselves to be short of time above everything else. Many of the principles set out in sections 4A and 4B apply after the meeting to individuals and groups with delegated responsibilities for team meetings. Certain strategies might be indicated according to the complexity of the project:

→ Milestones and key performance indicators – timelines with varying degrees of specificity.

→ Gantt charts for complex projects.

→ Links to the school improvement cycle/budgetary processes.

Perhaps the most potent strategy for ensuring impact following a decision making process is empowering people so that they feel trusted to make crucial decisions. This points to the importance of delegating genuine authority which is commensurate with the level of responsibility required to complete the task. Very often, authority in schools can lag behind responsibility and this inevitably compromises people's confidence to act and inhibits the development of leadership potential.

This raises two significant issues: first, decision making as a core leadership development strategy and, second, leadership decision making as a model for the classroom. There seems little doubt that one of the very best forms of leadership development is to be given the opportunity to actually lead – in essence, experiential learning. Seconding teachers and middle leaders to the leadership team, with a specific remit to launch an innovation or lead a small team to advise on a major project, is one of the most cost-effective means of development there is.

The other significant issue is that the greater the level of delegation of responsibility and authority to staff, the more likely it is that they, in turn, will delegate significant aspects of learning to their pupils. In both cases the school will move away from a dependency and permission seeking culture to one where trust is high, so there is real empowerment and respect for the dignity of each individual. Thus, effective leadership and management become models of effective learning and have the potential to inform changes in practice.

Try using resource 4C(i) to record the actions from your meeting. Do not record 'he says, she says' minute-by-minute accounts of the meeting; instead use the simple 'who, what, when' approach described above. At the start, agree who will be the achievability checker for the meeting – the one person who will check that the record is clear and the action is achievable. Everyone should agree at the end of each item, but who will check if it has been completed or not (don't always make this a senior colleague – develop trust and responsibility)? Make this record public, support each other and ensure that the meeting produces actions which are not only achievable but achieved. Success will breed success – when a meeting is approached with optimism it is far more likely to produce meaningful results.

The crucial concept here is subsidiarity: decisions should be taken at the lowest possible level by the people who are most affected by them.

Key questions

How successful is decision making in your school in terms of impact?

To what extent do school leadership meetings act as models of effective management, leadership and learning?

What strategies are in place to measure impact and to optimise the potential of time in meetings?

What training is available for school leaders and governors to optimise the effectiveness of meetings?

Resources (Download)

4C(i)   A pro forma for recording meeting actions

D   Optimising personal effectiveness

Why is this an important topic for conversation?

Effectiveness as a leader is directly contingent on personal effectiveness – it is impossible to divorce the leadership from the person. Therefore, personal effectiveness is a crucial antecedent to leadership effectiveness, and the ability to lead is made up of a range of personal qualities, behaviours and skills that cover the full spectrum of human interactions.

Key quotes for the section

> When people are in their Element, they connect with something fundamental to their sense of identity, purpose and well-being. Being there provides a sense of self-revelation, of defining who they really are and what they are meant to be doing with their lives.
>
> **(Robinson and Aronica, 2010: 21)**

> [Integrity] is what most people think about when they think of trust. To many, 'integrity' basically means 'honesty'. While integrity includes honesty, it's much more. It's integratedness. It's walking your talk. It's being congruent, inside and out. It's having the courage to act in accordance with your values and beliefs.
>
> **(Covey, 2006: 54)**

Section discussion

Personal effectiveness is largely a product of the ability to make decisions and then to act on them. The main criteria for effectiveness are the potential to complete a task, achieve an outcome or develop a relationship – in other words, to get things done. Thus, personal effectiveness is a combination of a range of complex variables that will change over time according to personal development and changing context. The most significant elements might be identified as follows:

→ Focus and clarity about your values and purpose, and the strategies to translate them into practice and adapt and modify them as appropriate. This focus also implies the ability to prioritise and define success criteria, which in turn implies confidence in translating principle into practice.

→ The confidence to act is significantly derived from robust personal review and self-knowledge based on openness to challenge and questioning, the ability to accept feedback and the capacity to genuinely learn from experience, and so change in an authentic way.

→ Personal effectiveness is as much about interaction as it is about introspection. Effectiveness is a product of emotional literacy – the ability to engage socially through positive relationships based on mutual trust and sophisticated interactions. This characteristic is often manifested in the ability to build rich networks and to work interdependently.

→ Personal effectiveness is often best manifested in terms of persistence and resilience – what is sometimes referred to as 'stickability', or the ability to keep going and bounce back when faced with adversity or negativity. This relates back to personal values and a strong sense of purpose, but it is also a manifestation of emotional maturity and well-developed strategies to make sense of negative challenges and frustration.

→ High performing individuals seem to have a different approach to stress. Crucially, stress is viewed not as being necessarily negative but rather, in some contexts, as positively beneficial. Good stress can reinforce focus, clarify issues and options and enhance energy and engagement. Negative stress can be highly damaging, both physically and psychologically. The key difference between positive stress and negative stress is the extent to which there is a sense of being in control and being able to exercise choice between appropriate alternatives – ultimately, the ability to say no.

→ Personal effectiveness is about a portfolio of skills and strategies – specific behaviours that increase the potential for control. In many ways, it is helpful to think of a range of skills that can be deployed according to the needs of a particular situation. For example:

  → The ability to prioritise, recognising the possible relationships between importance and urgency.

  → Having an analytical approach that focuses on strategic issues.

  → Using a range of problem solving tools and techniques.

→ Confidence in choosing between options.

→ Working with focused concentration/focusing on task completion.

→ Balancing work with relaxation across the day.

→ Developing boundaries to the demands of work.

→ The use of some mindfulness techniques, notably focused awareness on breathing, to control emotional responses.

→ Seeking and responding to feedback by using every opportunity to be open to suggestions for improvement and alternative ways of thinking and working. Such feedback might be obtained from a coach, mentor or critical friend. It is also about ending meetings with a short review and, if appropriate, using a tool such a SurveyMonkey questionnaire to capture more detailed and quantifiable data.

Use resource 4D(i) to complete a self-analysis of your own personal skill set and consider how effective you are. For each skill, consider how you use it and in what ways you could strengthen it.

Developing personal effectiveness is about a range of tools and techniques, but more fundamentally it is about personal fulfilment and authenticity. This is about working effectively, achieving personal well-being, being resilient and, crucially, sustaining personal optimism and hope. One way of understanding this is to think in terms of a reservoir of hope:

> The 'foundations of the reservoir of hope', the spiritual, moral and ethical bases on which individual leadership stands and which provide the well spring which motivates, replenishes and renews the capacity for spiritual and moral leadership, are provided by a clearly articulated value system which explicitly or implicitly underpins leadership actions by providing the reason why. (Flintham, 2010: 53)

We all know people whose reservoir seems to be permanently full – they have an energy and a resilience that is, quite frankly, exhausting! Equally, we know people whose reservoir is practically empty – they seem to limp through each day. One of the key characteristics of successful leadership in any aspect of education – from classroom to boardroom – is consistency, not least in the level of engagement, commitment and enthusiasm. It is not enough to be effective on 'good days'; that is why high performance leadership is so challenging.

Becoming personally effective and developing authenticity depends on the creation and nurturing of a reservoir of hope. Hope empowers us to take on new challenges, to make commitments, to trust and to approach the future with confidence. From hope comes courage and the desire to learn and grow. The reservoir is filled by creating time and space to focus on a sense of hope, optimism, peace and personal well-being. A full reservoir enables capacity and sustainability, but it needs to be nurtured and refilled. An empty reservoir leads to the loss of personal and professional effectiveness and authenticity.

The reservoir is replenished by a wide range of activities that nurture, refresh, inspire, reassure and engage us. Such activities may range from climbing a mountain to sailing a boat or singing in a choir, from engaging with personal faith to spending time with family and friends. Effective leaders know how deep their reservoir is and the best way to fill it. For some, the most helpful way of developing their personal repertoire of skills and sustaining high performance is by having a personal coach to support review and reflection, to identify ways forward and to monitor success. Resource 4D(ii) will help to shape your self-reflection around your ethos and the level of your reservoir of hope. Try to identify what you could do to boost the current level as well as trying to avoid things that will diminish it.

Key questions

How comfortable and confident are you in reviewing your personal effectiveness?

In terms of the skills of effective leaders, what steps have you taken to develop your personal portfolio, or do you rely on intuition?

How good are you at building support networks?

Have you tried working with a coach?

How do you replenish your reservoir?

Are you balancing your personal and professional effectiveness?

What are you doing about the effectiveness of your colleagues?

Resources (Download)

4D(i)   Investigating your skill set for personal effectiveness

4D(ii) Investigating your 'reservoir of hope'

4E

→ **E   High impact and low cost –
cost–benefit analysis in school management**

Why is this an important topic for conversation?

Whenever we make a major purchase in our personal lives we usually look for value for money – in other words, high quality for less cost. When working in the public sector there is a legal and moral imperative to spend public funds as wisely, effectively and efficiently as possible. The contraction in public sector finance means that these imperatives of value for money and appropriate expenditure have become even more important. In essence, for the first time in many years, schools are facing a significant decline in their income. The new culture that is needed has to focus on the principle of more for less.

One of the main implications is that budgetary decision making in schools may need to become much more rigorous and justifiable as the accountability model for expenditure becomes more stringent.

Key quote for the section

> [J]ust a few decades ago, best medical practice was driven by things like eminence, charisma, and personal experience. We needed the help of statisticians, epidemiologists, information librarians, and experts in trial design to move forwards. Many doctors – especially the most senior ones – fought hard against this, regarding 'evidence based medicine' as a challenge to their authority.
>
> In retrospect, we've seen that these doctors were wrong. The opportunity to make informed decisions about what works best, using good quality evidence, represents a truer form of professional independence than any senior figure barking out their opinions.
>
> **(Goldacre, 2013: 8)**

Section discussion

Most forms of professional activity involve choices: the ability to make appropriate choices is one of the key criteria for professional expertise and authority. Making prudent decisions which take account of a wide range of criteria is the central concern of Goldacre's study. Historically, decision making in schools might be caricatured as 'professional intuition' – that is, it is absolutely ethical in its approach but it may not be systematic or rigorous. For example, when buying textbooks the publisher's blurb will be read, as will endorsements from teachers who have used the book, but will the reading age of the resources be checked? As the pressure on schools' financial resources increase, so does the need for purchasing decisions to be fit for purpose (in the sense of maximum impact for minimum cost).

Here is a classic example of cost–benefit analysis – that is, the extent to which the claimed outcomes or benefits of a strategy actually justify the financial outlay. Baby simulators have been used in 89 countries as part of a strategy to reduce teenage pregnancy. The dolls provide a cautionary 24-hour experience in that they cry, 'urinate' and require 'feeding'. When asked by the government of Western Australia, prior to their introduction, if there was any evidence that the dolls actually led to a fall in pregnancy rates, the answer was that there was no valid or reliable evidence to justify the claims made. In fact, a subsequent rigorous study (Brinkman et al., 2016) of 2,800 girls in 57 schools found that girls who care for a doll may actually have higher rates of pregnancy and abortion. The dolls produce a range of outcomes but they don't actually work in terms of lowering rates of teenage pregnancy. The studies that claimed success for the product were largely based on short term satisfaction surveys rather than quantitative longitudinal studies based on randomised samples.

Very closely related to this approach is the concept of opportunity cost: if we buy the dolls, not only do they not work as claimed but we have used resources that might have been used to better effect. Cost–benefit analysis is deployed in a range of contexts – for example, in health it is used by the National Institute for Health and Care Excellence (NICE) to determine whether the cost of a drug or procedure is justified in terms of the impact on patients' health and well-being.

In an educational context, the best known example of a cost–benefit analysis approach is the Teaching and Learning Toolkit developed by the Sutton Trust and the EEF.[1] The purpose of the toolkit is to provide evidence on the most effective spending of the pupil premium. When first published the conclusions of the analysis were highly controversial because they challenged professional intuition – for example, the smaller the class size, the better or the more adults in a classroom, the better. Both are undoubtedly desirable from many perspectives but it seems they have relatively limited impact on the actual attainment of pupil premium students. The highest impact strategies – feedback, metacognitive development and homework in secondary schools and mastery learning

---

1   See https://educationendowmentfoundation.org.uk/resources/teaching-learning-toolkit.

reinforced by collaborative approaches – should, at least in theory, be the basis for most schools' approaches to working with pupil premium students. But we are not yet in the situation where decision making in education is evidence based.

An evaluation of the use of pupil premium funding (Cunningham and Lewis, 2012) found that the most commonly used strategies included early intervention schemes, reducing class sizes, more one-to-one tuition and additional teaching assistants – all of them problematic in terms of a cost–benefit approach. Just over half (52%) of the teachers surveyed said their school used past experience of what worked to decide which approaches and programmes to adopt to improve pupils' learning. However, only just over a third (36%) said their school used research evidence on the impact of different approaches and programmes:

> [L]arge proportions of teachers indicated that their school uses informal methods of evaluating approaches and programmes. These include trial-and-error approaches and learning from the experiences of other schools. While a large proportion of teachers believed that decisions in their school are based on research evidence, it is unclear what evidence they are using. (Cunningham and Lewis, 2012: 7)

Another area that is appropriate for a cost–benefit approach is continuing professional development (CPD), in particular the use of externally provided courses. They are attractive across a range of criteria but the outcomes can be at best fragile and at worst illusory. This is reinforced by the so-called 'evaluation sheets' handed out at the end of the day and usually faithfully completed. These are basically dressed-up satisfaction surveys along the lines of, 'Did you have a nice day?' Very rarely is there any follow-up looking for clear evidence that the course actually achieved its stated goals. Comments on 'a nice venue', 'interesting speaker' and a 'very good lunch' are unlikely to close the gap. Months would have to pass to assess the impact and there would need to be a trustworthy methodology in place to determine just what has changed and how much impact has been made in terms of pupil learning and attainment.

There are now more sources of trustworthy and authoritative evidence available to schools than ever before – for example, the Sutton Trust (www.suttontrust.com) and John Hattie's Visible Learning (https://visible-learning.org). However, we are some distance from evidence based school leadership and evidence informed classroom practice.

Possible strategies to improve this state of affairs might include:

→ Increasing the use of school data to inform key issues of resource management (e.g. teacher deployment).

→ School business managers developing networks to share data on the cost-effectiveness of resources.

→ Moving from CPD to joint practice development (JPD) (i.e. teacher led, classroom based learning such as lesson study).

→ Middle leaders, in particular, having responsibility for disseminating research as a part of team development.

→ Developing links with local universities to provide support for research based practice.

→ Starting a professional library.

→ Sharing data and good practice with other schools.

Use resource 4E(i) to look at how effective the approach to cost–benefit analysis is in your school. Clarify what is already done and consider how this could be strengthened.

Resource 4E(ii) is offered as a skeleton pro forma for use by staff for any spending in your school. It may well be considered unnecessary administration by some, but it is a system that could guard you against unnecessary levels of expenditure.

Key questions

> To what extent is decision making in your school based on objective and trustworthy evidence?

> Do you have clear protocols for the largest purchases?

> Does your school give value for money? How do you know?

> What proportion of professional practice in school is evidence based?

> How far have you moved from externally provided CPD to internally driven JPD?

> How many of your leadership team are research literate?

Resources (Download)

4E(i) Considering the strategies used to improve cost–benefit analysis in your school

4E(ii) A cost–benefit pro forma to assess spending in your school

Learning and technology

A   Will the genie go back in the bottle?

Why is this an important topic for conversation?

The growth of information communication technology (ICT) is not some passing fad. Digital communication has changed the way individuals think and react to the world around them. School is the formal organisation of a nation's learning, so it would seem obvious that these changes in approach should be fully represented in classrooms.

However, in many schools electronic devices are regarded simply as gadgets, while in others they have become the enemy. There is no doubt that the advent of ICT poses many problems for schools, from the ease of access to information (falsehoods and facts) to cyber-bullying and exploitation. It is equally clear that burying your head in the sand and hoping it will go away is not an option.

Key quotes for the section

> Children no longer need to see their teachers as the font of all knowledge. In fact, they know they are not. Instead, they need to see their teachers as modellers of learning, master learners, risk-takers, facilitators, collaborators, creators and, to top it all, those teachers have to be tech-savvy. In today's child's world, content, knowledge and teachers are everywhere and accessible at all times. As educators, we have to change, and we should be excited about embracing the challenge and reaping the rewards.
>
> **(Pridham, 2014: 2)**

> [C]omputers embody the double binds experienced by the cultures that created them and that are now giving them a central role in the messianic project of modernisation. Because a double bind encompasses both benefits and drawbacks, and because we usually focus only on the benefits, the drawbacks often go unnoticed. For example, the Industrial Revolution raised the material standard of living and brought many conveniences into the lives of ordinary people; but its success depended on the destruction of self-sufficient and symbolically rich cultures, turned much of the environment into a wasteland, and put the world on its current environmentally destructive pathway.
>
> **(Bowers, 2011: 1)**

> I think it's fair to say that personal computers have become the most empowering tool we've ever created. They're tools of communication, they're tools of creativity, and they can be shaped by their user.
>
> **(Gates, 2014)**

> Computers are useless. They can only give you answers.
>
> **(attributed to Pablo Picasso)**

Section discussion

For many currently working in education, the school is the sole focus of their day. Many complain that they have no time to think, that the school becomes their life. It is therefore unsurprising that advances in technology seem to have left some classrooms behind. One hundred years ago most areas of the world had clarity of expectations for their schools: the teacher's role was to be more learned than the pupils in front of them and through a series of lessons to impart some of that knowledge to them. The teacher could show the pupils a list of the five longest rivers in the world, ask them to copy them down, memorise them and then test them at the end of the week. The teacher pats herself on the back and then goes home, secure in the knowledge of a job well done. The role of a teacher was achievable.

The fact that today's classroom is not the same as it was at the turn of the 20th century may be an obvious one, but it appears to have been forgotten by some. Resource 5A(i) may be a useful prequel to a longer discussion about what we want from our classrooms now. It shows a classroom from a century ago and encourages the identification of practices and structures that the modern classroom would want to keep, as well as ones that may need rethinking. The reality is that there has been a sea change in the way modern civilisation is constructed: we are no longer an industrial society.

Fundamental changes like this are rare, but they have a profound effect on citizens. In the 18th century, the shift from an agricultural to an industrial society was accompanied by huge social upheaval: populations shifted from the countryside to new urban centres, families were split up and cultural values were transformed. Unsurprisingly, this resulted in a 50 year spike in health related issues (including suicide). There is a general acceptance that we are now moving towards being a post-industrial society, which some refer to as the communication or information society; however it is labelled, though, the challenge to our education system is at least as profound as those in previous transformations.

Given that we appear to be in a turbulent period of transition, it is disappointing (but not surprising) that education remains wedded to a school system designed and operated for success in a different type of society. The current rate of industrial change is rapid, but fast change does not suit our model of schooling. For example, most schools still focus their success on exam performance. Exams are based on a syllabus, and in many cases that syllabus is rooted on the one before that. Any change to the syllabus will inevitably take a number of years, then the course will fill a further two years before an examination is possible. This mentality encourages the preservation of the status quo.

One of the biggest frustrations voiced by school leaders is that they feel like victims of other people's decisions and priorities. This may indeed be a valid moan; however, in times of rapid change the school leader's role becomes even more important. It is not to simply fulfil the requirements placed on them by government but also to challenge the whole environment in which schools operate. School leaders working with their local community to clarify what is needed from the education system not only helps the work inside the school, but it also helps the wider community that the school serves to understand the changes they are facing.

It would be easy to dismiss this topic as inconsequential or abstract. In fact, helping to position your school to support the changes faced by society, rather than propagate old thinking, could be one of the most important things you do. Resource 5A(ii) would make a good focus for your leadership team to investigate how you are responding to the challenges posed by a new type of society and to clarify the exact purpose of your school within it. Complete the resource in advance of the meeting and then use the discussion to explore ways in which your current approach is still rooted in the assumptions of an industrial society. Identify changes that you could be making to the activities of the school, even if you are not yet confident how you will do them. Where you detect practices which are actually counter to the direction in which the school should be heading, highlight them with staff, pupils and parents, making sure everyone understands why you are still doing this and encourage them to make their voices heard in driving change.

Many schools are clear that they would like to put the genie back in the bottle and revert back to an age pre-computers. Anyone who has experienced the frustrations and upset caused around pupils' misuse of social media will probably be leading this call – there is no doubt that new technologies have brought a very dark side with them which any rational person would like to remove from our schools. However, the benefits are equally clear: the instant availability of information, ideas and art from anywhere in the world is surely too valuable to be ignored. And isn't it more important to become a centre of learning, for it is clearly the role of schools to ensure that all pupils are able to use the equipment and information around them to maximise their future potential?

Key questions

Why do you do what you do?

How much of what you do is passed on from a previous time?

Have you discussed why you are doing what you do?

How do you balance the benefits and dangers of new digital technologies?

Have you currently got that balance right?

Resources (Download)

5A(i) Prompting discussion about the comparisons between classrooms of the past and present

5A(ii) Identifying how schools are responding to the challenges of a post-industrial society

B   The great mobile phone debate – learning tool vs. distraction

Why is this an important topic for conversation?

According to the GMSA (2017), the number of mobile phone users in the world has increased year on year and by 2020 is expected to reach five billion. One of the most rapidly growing sub-groups of users is children, with increasing numbers of children owning mobile phones even in primary schools. This is fact. What is open to debate is what schools should do in response. Are smartphones 'windows on the world' – high-tech learning devices that should be key to children's education – or are they dangerous weapons that can obstruct children's learning and make the classroom a less safe environment? Or something in-between?

Key quotes for the section

> Students have also found a great use of cell phones and most of them go with their cell phones to school. Cell phones are not bad or harmful as some educators can think, but the problem is that some students use them for [the] wrong reasons and this makes them bad in school. Since most cell phones now[a]days can access [the] internet, students tend to use them for selfish entertaining reasons while in the classroom, this creates distraction and it also affects [their] grades.
>
> **(Ramey, 2012)**

> Schools generally grapple with new technologies, but cell phones' reputation as a nuisance and a distraction has been hard to dislodge.
>
> Recently, however, the acceptance of these devices has been growing. Beginning in March, New York City, the largest school district in the country with 1.1 million students, will reverse its long standing ban on cell phones in schools.
>
> **(Kiema, 2015)**

> Banning mobile phones improves outcomes for the low-achieving students (14.23% of a standard deviation) the most and has no significant impact on high achievers. The results suggest that low-achieving students are more likely to be distracted by the presence of mobile phones, while high achievers can focus in the classroom regardless of whether phones are present.
>
> **(Beland and Murphy, 2015: 3)**

> Every time there's a new tool, whether it's Internet or cell phones or anything else, all these things can be used for good or evil. Technology is neutral; it depends on how it's used.
>
> **(Smolan, 2013)**

Section discussion

Two pupils in neighbouring schools can have very different experiences in how they are able to use their mobile phone at school.

School A has recently adopted a 'zero tolerance' approach towards mobile phones. Any pupil found carrying a phone has it removed and placed in a safe place – it can only be retrieved by meeting with a parent. The school claims that this action, once embedded, has had a very positive effect on pupil behaviour in the school. In addition, the leadership team have read the paper from the Centre for Economic Performance (Beland and Murphy, 2015) and hope that exam results will also improve as a result of this strategy. The pastoral teams in the school report that they are seeing a reduction in the frequency of cyber related bullying issues and believe that the action is making their pupils safer.

School B has decided to encourage pupils to use their mobile phones in school. The reasons for their decision were multifold: (1) they were finding that confiscation of phones was a cause of conflict, not just with pupils but also with some parents who wanted their child to have their phone with them to ensure they were safe when travelling home; (2) they feel it is their role to educate pupils in the correct and safe use of mobile phones; (3) they see this as a low cost way of increasing the number of Internet-ready devices that pupils have access to; and (4) they want pupils to use the cameras on their phones to capture their work in development.

5B

Both schools claim to be happy with their approach and point to evidence that it is the right way forward. Use resource 5B(i) to focus discussion on the relative merits of the two scenarios. Some of the focus may overlap but considering each scenario from the perspective of pupils, staff and parents will ensure the discussion is a wide one. Decide where your own school approach fits in the debate – are you closer to school A or B? Are you happy with your current position? If you don't think your policy is correct for your pupils, use the discussion to explore a hybrid version of the two positions that suits your school. Use resource 5B(ii) to scope out a position between A and B by highlighting key advantages and disadvantages of the two extremes.

There are examples of schools on both sides of the debate who demonstrate how their current position works for them. It is clear that mobile phones can be a damaging distraction to learning and, equally, they can be a powerful tool to engage pupils in learning. Whatever the adopted position of your school, even if it currently suits your needs very well, it is unlikely that this will always be the case. As the demands on education (and therefore educators) change over the coming years, this is an issue you are going to need to constantly review. Every week, new features and new distractions are added to mobile devices. The phone's utility has shifted from being mainly a tool of voice communication to a powerful mobile computer. With the advent of imaginative apps, a phone can be transformed into a data collector, a digital microscope, an instant translator, a sketchpad, a notebook, a thesaurus, a grammar checker, a mapping tool and so much more. Most school principals, if presented with the opportunity to have a free digital learning tool of such varied usefulness for use by every pupil, wouldn't have to think twice before accepting it. However, as we know, these benefits are accompanied by some very concerning negatives; the potential for remote bullying or exploitation, the ability to access false or even salacious information, the facility to take or receive invasive photographs and the potential for distraction by addictive games. These concerns should not be ignored by schools, but equally these issues are not removed from a pupil's life simply by banning phones from school premises.

The long term future for the development of mobile phones in schools must surely be to work on developing pupils' skills in using the technology safely and wisely. Schools around the world are finding ways to balance the two sides of the problem by trying to curb the negatives while embracing the positives. Resource 5B(iii) contains some examples of what teachers are successfully using mobile phones for in the classroom. The list is not exhaustive but it is intended as a discussion point to provoke your own thinking.

Key questions

What percentage of your pupils own mobile phones?

What is your school policy on using them to support learning?

How do you curb the negatives of their use?

How do you promote the positives they offer?

Resources (Download)

5B(i)   Comparing the approach to mobile phones in two schools
5B(ii) Investigating a hybrid solution to mobile phone use in schools
5B(iii) Some ways that schools are using mobile phones in the classroom

5C

C   Educating the digital generation – digital natives

Why is this an important topic for conversation?

From the moment the current generation of school pupils open their eyes in the morning to the moment they close them at night, their experience of – and relationship with – technology is completely different to that of previous generations. Marc Prensky wrote a key article on the topic in 2001 in which he introduced the evocative phrases 'digital native' and 'digital immigrant', which are still used but contentious. Even at that time, he was pointing out that the digital immigrant educators had a serious challenge to cope with: they were unable to understand the new world they were working in as well as the digital natives for whom they had responsibility to teach. Since then, the digital world has developed in ways no one could have predicted and many teachers have endeavoured to bridge the digital divide themselves. While the situation is not so clearly delineated as it was in 2001 when Prensky wrote his article, the underlying issue is still a crucial one for schools to address.

Key quotes for the section

> So, more correctly than as a specific digital generation, these developments can best be described as a transitional phase where digital media are still in transition and where young people today are experiencing a dual culture, between the old and the new.
>
> **(Erstad, 2010)**

> The new digital world is having a profound impact on modern students. They actually think differently than older people who did not grow up in the digital environment. Educators must adapt their approaches to instruction and the organization of their schools to address this new reality if they hope to engage students in learning today and into the future.
>
> **(Kelly et al., 2009: 5)**

> " Despite what you hear occasionally in the media, there really is no such thing as a 'digital native' – everyone, regardless of whether they are a baby boomer, Millennial or the next generation sometimes referred to as 'Gen Z', must start from somewhere.
>
> **(Britland, 2016)** "

Section discussion

If the parent of a prospective pupil asks you, on visiting your school, 'What about computers? Do all your teachers use the latest technologies?' how would you respond? If you answer, 'We have the latest technologies here – every class has an interactive board,' you may be unintentionally avoiding the real issue: the level of teacher experience in using technology to enhance learning. The highest specification classroom tool may be less effective than much simpler (and cheaper) examples in the hands of an educator who is more digitally competent.

When a school is looking to modernise its educational provision, leaders will often reach first for the latest catalogue from a top educational provider. However, this is unlikely to be the best use of your resources. A wise first move for a leadership team is to carry out a staff review of ICT confidence.

Here is flowchart to help you with this process:

Teacher confidence in the use of technology

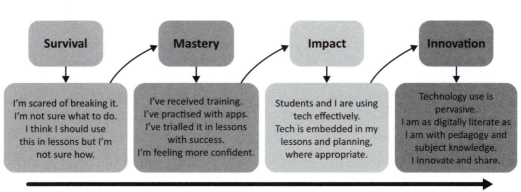

Confidence/competence

Source: Anderson (2013), based on the work of Mandinach and Cline (1993).

Use resource 5C(i) to find out about levels of ICT confidence from your teaching staff, and use resource 5C(ii) to collate this information. Once you have collected data about levels of self-confidence it is important for these views to be moderated by the ICT leader. Some staff may be reluctant to label themselves as 'survival' even though the descriptor suits them, with some even exhibiting signs of a phobia if signalling a need for support may cause them to have to face this fear. At the other end of the confidence scale, some staff will be reluctant to place an 'innovation' label on their heads, either because they understand what they don't know or because they realise that the label may result in an increased workload. Resource 5C(ii) therefore has a column for the leader with the most sophisticated view of technology to complete.

Once you have a clearer view of the technological profile of your staff it is imperative to ask the question: is this profile the one we need in order to help our pupils learn over the coming years? Most schools do not have the luxury of answering yes to this question, recognising that the technological confidence level of some of their staff is not where it should be to support future learners. The high workload of most teachers means this problem is not easily overcome: many will understandably talk about priorities and see developing technological competency as an unwanted 'extra'. Schools that foster coaching partnerships among their staff are more likely to see this profile improve. Linking up teachers with different levels of expertise can encourage them to work together, which is less threatening than didactic instruction, and will help less confident teachers to understand the advantages of using technology to support learning.

It is important for school leaders to promote positive discussion about the changing needs of the education of digital natives as the engagement with technology develops, thereby ensuring that the discussion does not adopt the traditionalist stance of 'the youth of today can't concentrate'. Neuroscientists believe that there has been little change in brain structure over the past 10,000 years (in fact, some scientists believe that the human brain has shrunk in that time),[1] so to suggest that using technology has somehow changed the nature of children's brains seems unlikely. However, it is reasonable to consider the social effect that technology has had on the way children interact with the world around them; the people, the information and the learning. They don't expect their teachers to know everything because they are used to finding out information in entertaining ways. Perhaps technology has not changed the brain but it has changed expectations: children do not expect learning to be sterile.

---

1   See https://www.scientificamerican.com/article/how-has-human-brain-evolved/.

There is a dazzling array of examples on the Internet of schools that are using technology imaginatively to support the learning of their pupils. Each day, new software and hardware become available, and the schools that use it best are those with high levels of staff in the 'innovation' category. Encourage discussion among your staff about new developments, set up a development noticeboard in the staffroom, share some of the top ICT related blogs and, above all, encourage staff to take risks with technology!

Some ICT related blogs which contain useful up-to-date information are:

https://ictevangelist.com/
https://theinnovativeeducator.blogspot.co.uk/
http://www.freetech4teachers.com/
http://www.gizmodo.co.uk/

Key questions

What is the current level of ICT self-confidence among your staff?

How is this limiting the development of your school?

Can you improve the profile by coaching?

Do you look for and share the latest developments in this area?

Resources (Download)

5C(i)	Increasing confidence in the use of technology
5C(ii)	Summarising staff confidence in ICT

D   Maximising the effective use of the ICT budget

Why is this an important topic for conversation?

In the 1960s lasers were in the realms of science fiction. Today they are found in every home, most cars, in DIY stores and at supermarket checkouts. They have become commonplace. So too with information and communications technology. The ubiquity of tablets points to a radical realignment in our access to information, the management of that information and its subsequent deployment. Information technology is already demonstrating the potential to call into question just about every historic assumption about the what, where, when, how and who of learning – just as it is transforming virtually every other aspect of our lives.

Key quotes for the section

> The most important pillar behind innovation and opportunity – education – will see tremendous positive change in the coming decades as rising connectivity reshapes traditional routines and offers new paths for learning. Most students will be highly technologically literate, as schools continue to integrate technology into lesson plans and, in some cases, replace traditional lessons with more interactive workshops. Education will be a more flexible experience.
>
> **(Schmidt and Cohen, 2013: 21)**

> [T]he problem with technology is twofold: the digital world of the student is largely outside schools, and it is essentially undisciplined – all over the multi-tasking map ... By far the greater problem is the gross underutilization of mobile devices.
>
> **(Fullan, 2013: 71)**

Section discussion

Interactive whiteboards were once hailed as the most significant and transformational resource in the classroom. In the hands of a skilled teacher they could be truly awe-inspiring in terms of their creativity, impact on learning and pupil engagement. However, for a range of reasons many whiteboards have become rather sophisticated chalkboards. Their usage does not justify the cost and their potential is not being realised. One reason may be the simple fact that they are essentially static – the board occupies a space in the classroom that reinforces traditional modes of working: the class sitting facing the teacher and the media. Only the colour of the board has changed.

Back in the 1970s, Moore's law correctly predicted that the power of computers would double every year or so. This has meant that ever more powerful computers have cost less and less money. The rate may be slowing, but it is likely that we will continue to see lower prices and increasing power for some time to come. The variety and power of phones and tablets have transformed personal communication. It is not unusual to see families out for a meal all using their devices; equally, virtually everyone on a train will be using some form of personal computing.

As Michael Fullan observes, there is no shortage of devices in schools – they are simply not being used appropriately. At the same time, resources to go with all the new hardware are beginning to emerge. There are increasing numbers of schools addressing this issue, one of the best examples being the Khan Academy (www.khanacademy.org), which provides a wide range of short courses that seem to have a very positive impact on students' understanding and engagement.

The key issues in terms of using ICT to manage resources in the school would seem to be:

→ Ensuring that all staff (whatever their personal convictions) are fully competent in the use of ICT as is appropriate to their role. For high impact and cost-effectiveness this training could be done by students.

→ Secondary schools collaborating with primaries to make sure that all pupils have the appropriate ICT skills.

→ Working to ensure that the school moves towards being paperless (e.g. no printed agendas/papers for meetings, CPD hand-outs or school policies). Photocopying to be reduced by 75% in the first year.

→ Developing a strategy to reuse outdated e-readers to support literacy strategies.

→ Giving all staff a tablet or compensating them for using their own.

→ Working with other schools and further education/higher education institutions to establish community businesses that will upgrade, refurbish and repair tablets to ensure that all students have their own.

→ Establishing a partnership with other schools to develop virtual textbooks, thus eliminating the expense of replacing out-of-date books while also developing resources better suited to the needs of the students and the school's curriculum.

→ Developing school based research to monitor and evaluate the most successful applications and disseminate them.

→ Increasing and enhancing communication with parents through texting.

Resource 5D(i) is a tabular form of the above list which invites you to consider your school's successes in that area and the ways in which your work could be improved.

Electronic textbooks raise some interesting issues because in many ways they encapsulate lots of the changes required in terms of culture and professional practice. Possible advantages include:

→ They can be updated on a regular basis as new material becomes available (e.g. publishers develop more resources that can be downloaded).

→ Teachers are able to control issues such as readability and presentation.

→ The most successful lessons can be filmed and made available permanently.

→ Successful work by students can be incorporated into the resource.

→ Links can be made to MOOCs (massive open online courses) and SPOCs (small private open/online courses).

Another consequence of schools producing their own materials by drawing on the Internet's vast supply of resources that are free of copyright is the potential for personalisation and for individuals and groups of students to develop their own resources as part of the learning process.

Use resource 5D(ii) to encourage all staff to evaluate any potential ICT resource. The form should be collected centrally and considered by a group whose role it is to monitor the ICT budget. The more the staff (and possibly the pupils) are involved in considering possibilities, the greater the potential benefit they offer.

Key questions

How would you categorise your school in terms of readiness and confidence to engage with technological change?

To what extent are school leaders modelling the changes necessary?

To what extent is the advice of students being sought?

What work has been done to evaluate the cost-effectiveness of existing patterns of ICT provision?

Resources (Download)

5D(i)	Evaluating the key factors that ensure effective use of ICT budgets
5D(ii)	Considering the potential of online materials

E   Using technology to enhance leadership

Why is this an important topic for conversation?

The information technology revolution is about the management of information – it's as simple and complex as that. By the same token, leadership is about making decisions and exercising choices. However, it would be naive to pretend that developments in technology will not be reflected to a significant extent in the ways in which schools function.

Key quotes for the section

> Leadership is desperately needed in education today to bring about the shift in instruction that is urgently required to keep students engaged in learning and to prepare them for success in the future. It will require courage to take the leadership that is needed because leading education into the 21st century will mean going against the grain with fellow educators. It will mean going against the long-standing mindset for what teaching and learning looks like by diving into the new digital world to gain the experience needed to critically assess the value of new ways to communicate with others, to entertain ourselves, to perform work both by ourselves and collaboratively with others, and to assess the relative value of new online digital experiences with traditional non-digital ones.
>
> **(Jukes et al., 2010: 135)**

> Technology has just as much evil or good as we want to put into it. That is why we need pedagogy and the moral imperative to be the key drivers. … Leadership needs to become the ultimate cohesive driver. … Leaders then must foster in others the capacity to focus, to innovate, to empathize, to learn, to collaborate, to relish transparency, to shed non-essentials and to develop leadership in themselves and others. Ultimately, everyone becomes a change agent.
>
> **(Fullan, 2013: 71)**

Section discussion

Think about the checkout at your local supermarket. It is a combination of lasers reading barcodes and computerised details of what you have purchased and the cost of each item. In fact, the checkout is an extremely sophisticated intelligence system that allows the store manager to identify trends in the demand, provide continuous data to ensure that appropriate orders are sent to the warehouse, identify patterns of customer activity to help with staff deployment, develop profiles of customers with loyalty cards to inform targeted advertising campaigns and changes in levels of expenditure, and test the success of new lines.

Thus, the hard data becomes a sophisticated and highly reliable knowledge base that informs strategic leadership decisions. In the same way, some garages are now filming certain procedures used during car servicing and emailing them to the customer as evidence of the garage's integrity and performance.

Most schools are now data rich; however, as we have seen, they are not always evidence based in their policies or practice. A central issue for school leaders is managing the tension between competing sets of cultural norms and expectations – in essence, the alternative perspectives offered by the traditional educationalists and the emerging digital generation. A useful example of this tension is the secondary textbook – usually expensive, often with a relatively short shelf life and almost never entirely right for the class that will be using it. One answer to this problem is the development, by teachers, of their own electronic textbooks. They can make the resource bespoke to their course and incorporate a wide range of sources so the text is up to date, includes examples of students' work from previous years and is available on tablets for individual use. Medium and message would both be fit for purpose and money would be saved.

Applying the same broad principle of using ICT to improve rather than replace, there seems little doubt that a range of traditional leadership functions can be significantly enhanced by the application of new technologies. Such functions might include the leadership of learning – in particular, securing equity by embedding consistency, monitoring and maintaining high performance, improving communication and deploying staff to optimal effect.

→ *Learning.* Wide access to information offers the possibility of moving education from the dominant experience of transmission of information towards a more collaborative problem solving approach whereby learners become self-managing. Equally, the potential for personalising education to respond to needs and talents is significantly enhanced through access to appropriate online resources (e.g. MOOCs and SPOCs) and provisions such as the Khan Academy and FutureLearn.

→ *Consistency*. Securing parity of provision is the basis for equity and quality in education. Variation is a challenge facing many leaders, but ICT provides the means to ensure greater levels of consistency over time – and across the school – by establishing and disseminating best practice, ensuring access to quality resources, maintaining consistent assessment and supporting teachers' review and reflection.

→ *Monitoring performance*. Data is only of value to the extent to which it moves beyond description into analysis and then to intervention. School based data gives teachers, team leaders, senior leaders and governors the evidence necessary to identify the most appropriate intervention strategies and then to assess their impact and effectiveness. In many schools the iPad, containing all of the school's performance data, has become the essential senior leadership accessory.

→ *Communication*. Although there is a very strong case for outlawing sending emails to anyone who is within 100 yards, or sending messages during lesson time, ICT has the potential to significantly enhance the quality of communication in schools. At the very least, the open circulation of documents (with appropriate opportunities for response) could see a number of meetings being cancelled, thus freeing time for higher order interactions.

→ *Deploying staff*. There is abundant evidence (e.g. the research and resources of the EEF and Sutton Trust) that one of the most powerful ways of securing progress for all pupils, but the most disadvantaged in particular, is the appropriate deployment of staff. The utilisation of staff needs to be on the basis of demonstrated effectiveness rather than personal wishes or historical precedent.

Resource 5E(i) gives you a simple table to help you consider your current use of ICT across the different facets of leadership. For each area, consider the ways in which your current use causes a problem and find ways to reduce this.

A further possible application for ICT in leadership, one that may not work for all leaders but is a powerful version of a well-proven technique, is to support review and reflection (e.g. keeping an electronic journal, researching alternative opinions, hypothesising). For some, reflective writing is a very powerful technique to support development and structured analysis when working with a coach or mentor.

Resource 5E(ii) will appeal to some leaders as a template for promoting reflective thinking. For some a more open diary form will be preferred, but for others this template can be used as a prompt to reflect on the highs and lows of the day. Used frequently, this could be of great assistance in collecting your thoughts on a busy day and helping you to form your leadership priorities.

Key questions

What is your fundamental response to the challenges offered by ICT?

Do you see yourself as an 'early adopter' or are you more cautious?

Do you model the uses of technology that you advocate in your school?

To what extent have your school values guided and directed your school's ICT policies and strategies?

What is the strategic thinking about the medium term impact of ICT on teaching and learning in your school?

Resources (Download)

5E(i)   Thinking about how you use technology in your leadership
5E(ii)   Reflective thinking

Education beyond the school

A   What can we learn from education around the world?

Why is this an important topic for conversation?

Education is a fundamental part of every society in the world. All nations want to ensure that their future citizens are able to play an important role in the development of their country. The logic goes like this: we want our children to be the best educated in the world, therefore they will grow into the most well-informed and active citizens in the world, resulting in us becoming a successful country. The weakness of this logic is its simplicity: just because a society is fixated on assessment outcomes (i.e. ensuring children are effective test completers) does not guarantee that these systems are effective and successful. Indeed, the current obsession of many countries to compete in a PISA league table battle may well be counterproductive in the long term. The increase in young people's mental health problems due to a relentless focus on testing is unlikely to produce robust and adaptable citizens in the best position to help their country adapt to the changing world around them.

Key quotes for the section

> Finland is regarded as one of the world's most literate societies. As a nation of modest people, Finland never actually intended to be the best in the world. Finns like to compete, but *collaboration* is a more typical characteristic of this nation.
>
> **(Sahlberg, 2012: 1; original emphasis)**

> In a stable, unchanging world, decisions that worked before can be made again without understanding why they work. However, in a changing world, tradition no longer provides security. Choices have to be made with respect to which perspectives to pursue in which sequence, the combinations of physical and financial resources that are required and the people to use and manage those resources, how long the effort should be made, and how to tell when the effort is failing and should be corrected or has succeeded and can be terminated. These decisions are most likely to be correct and result in the desired outcomes when they are based on a correct and comprehensive understanding of the current and future situations and of the organization itself.
>
> **(Reimers and McGinn, 1997: 4)**

> Every country should conduct its own reforms, should develop its own model, taking into account the experience of other countries, whether close neighbours or far away countries.
>
> **(Mikhail Gorbachev, quoted in PBS, 2001)**

> One of the things I'm fascinated by as a traveler is watching how different countries control how they let the world encounter them.
>
> **(Hanya Yanagihara, quoted in *Vogue*, 2013)**

Section discussion

It has become quite common to hear of head teachers (and their political masters) travelling to exotic locations on 'fact finding' tours (one can only assume the exotic part of the chosen location is a mere coincidence!). There can be little doubt that opening yourself up to how different countries approach the education of their young people can be a transformational experience. As described in the quote from Fernando Reimers and Noel McGinn, in times of change it is simply not enough to keep trying the same things that used to work. Although each country is operating within the same larger global community, the precise local conditions are unique to each nation; even though the experience may be similar, there will be subtle differences which make direct comparison almost impossible. Nevertheless, it can be very useful to see how certain strategies are used to cope, successfully or otherwise, with particular challenges.

A recurring problem is when individuals (often politicians) return from a visit to a country with a 'good reputation' armed with 'the answer'. At best this is naive, at worst dangerous. To spend a few hours at a school, identify some differences and then make judgements on the totality of the school's success is foolish. For example, you might visit a highly acclaimed school with a very smart uniform – a school where the leaders attribute the introduction of the uniform as a key factor in their subsequent improvement – and return absolutely certain that introducing a new uniform should be your main priority. However, you could also visit another highly acclaimed school where the leaders identify a lack of uniform as the secret to their success. So who is right? The answer is probably both!

This is the difficulty with any type of inter-school comparison – it is often not 'what is done' but 'how it is done' that is most enlightening. And it is usually not the obvious differences that are the most interesting (start time of the day, lesson length, class numbers, finance, etc.) but rather the leadership approach and the reasons why the school does what it does.

Geoff Moorcroft, director of education on the Isle of Man (an island with a small, independent education system), identified in a recent document for visiting school leaders the value of focusing on the relationships in the school they visit:

> Relationships within organisations are fundamentally important. Head teachers need to unlock the potential of people within their organisations by distributing real leadership opportunities to them and those of us who work centrally need to do the same. We seek, wherever possible, to work collaboratively with schools and school leaders. Senior leaders can do much to build and strengthen capacity for themselves and their staff through ambitious collaboration and deep partnerships with others to undertake robust action research into local issues. As David Hargreaves puts it, a self-sustaining school system would 'usher in a new era in which the school system becomes the major agent of its own improvement and does so at a rate and to a depth that has hitherto been no more than an aspiration'. (internal publication, quoting Hargreaves, 2010: 4)

So, perhaps the most important idea we can take away from observing the practice of other schools is how they cope with the changes they face in the local/national environment. A core unifying factor between schools, even those in very different circumstances, is the commonality of facing a world where the future is no longer predictable. When visiting other schools (whether in your own country or on a different continent), look for areas of learning around the way school leaders interact with the world around them – use resource 6A(i) to focus your thoughts. Identify the challenges that are unique to your own school and the visited school, and place these in the appropriate sets in the top half of the Venn diagram, noting the common or similar challenges in the overlapping section. Then concentrate on the solutions being used to solve the problem, again noting the differences on both sides and those held in common in the overlapping section in the lower half of the diagram.

Resource 6A(ii) is offered as a mechanism to focus on the relationships and leadership actions you observe in a visited school and to consider their transferability to your own school's situation. Initially, centre your thinking on some strategic issues (ideally relevant to your own school) that the visited school is trying to address. For each one identify the key relationships that have been necessary to develop the solution and the actions they have made to embed this. This will then enable you to identify approaches that might be appropriate to your own circumstances.

The huge diversity of schooling in one country, let alone across the globe, means you will find both successful and unsuccessful schools for almost any scenario, be it the length of the school day, subjects covered, teaching styles used, use of technology or any one of thousands of other variables. Maximum benefit will be obtained not by searching for specific solutions (e.g. does a short lunchtime work?) but by identifying how other schools have addressed a similar problem (e.g. more challenging pupil behaviour in the afternoon).

Seeing how others approach problems is always interesting, but you should never lose sight of the uniqueness of your own school and community and the need to grow your own individual solution from this starting point.

Key questions

What problems are you trying to solve?

Where else in the world might schools have similar issues to solve?

What relationships have been important in the solutions they have found?

How do you need to adapt the approach for your own context?

Resources (Download)

6A(i)	A Venn diagram for comparing your school with another school
6A(ii)	Recognising the transferable learning from a visit to another school

6B

B   Citizenship for the 21st century

Why is this an important topic for conversation?

The pivotal issue for this section is where the boundaries of education are. Does education only consist of school based studies focused on academic subjects, or do schools have a wider remit – notably, preparing young people for life after school, not just in terms of employability but also living a meaningful life in wider society and contributing towards sustaining democracy?

Key quotes for the section

> Teaching as a profession is closely tied to sustaining Finnish national culture and building an open and multicultural society. Indeed, one purpose of formal schooling is to transfer cultural heritage, values, and aspirations from one generation to another. Teachers are, according to their own opinions, essential players in building the Finnish welfare society.
>
> **(Sahlberg, 2015: 100)**

> Never doubt that a small group of thoughtful, committed citizens can change the world; indeed, it's the only thing that ever has.
>
> **(Anon.)**

Section discussion

The prevailing social-democratic consensus of western and developed world governments that emerged after the Second World War is today being challenged in ways that seemed unthinkable even just a few years ago. It appears that many voters are increasingly disillusioned with the centrist parties that have been dominant during this period and are shifting their allegiance to neoliberal and populist parties.

Part of the response of the British government has been to stress the importance of British values in social education and across the curriculum. According to Ofsted (2016: 35–36), British values include democracy, the rule of law, individual liberty and mutual respect for, and tolerance of, those with different faiths and beliefs and for those without faith. It is important to note, as an antidote to the rejection of international engagement, that these are not just British values – they are human values that have served as the basis for societies for many years.

This classically liberal stance is deeply embedded in our norms and institutions, but appears to be under threat in a world that is becoming increasingly intolerant of difference. For the Department for Education (2014: 5), the 'core values' in education can be translated into the following components:

→ *enable students to develop their self-knowledge, self-esteem and self-confidence;*

→ *enable students to distinguish right from wrong and to respect the civil and criminal law of England;*

→ *encourage students to accept responsibility for their behaviour, show initiative, and to understand how they can contribute positively to the lives of those living and working in the locality of the school and to society more widely;*

→ *enable students to acquire a broad general knowledge of and respect for public institutions and services in England;*

→ *further tolerance and harmony between different cultural traditions by enabling students to acquire an appreciation of and respect for their own and other cultures;*

→ *encourage respect for other people; and*

→ *encourage respect for democracy and support for participation in the democratic processes, including respect for the basis on which the law is made and applied in England.*

Resource 6B(i) is offered as a way of analysing your own school's practice with respect to the development of citizenship skills. On this basis, citizenship is not just about knowing British values and not working against them, but rather is about active engagement in seeking to understand those values and working to develop them in practice.

Citizenship development in schools is not just teaching about British values in order to pass a 'Know Your Britain' style quiz. Instead, it needs to be approached in two ways: first, to develop understanding through debate, enquiry, questioning, challenge and thinking and, second, it would be hypocritical in the extreme to teach British values if they are not actually embedded in the life of the school. A very successful example of this approach is exemplified in the Rights Respecting School Award (RRSA):

[F]or the majority, the values based on the United Nations Convention on the Rights of the Child (CRC) and 'guide to life' provided by the RRSA (Rights

Respecting School Award) has had a significant and positive influence on the school ethos, relationships, inclusivity, understanding of the wider world and the well-being of the school community, according to the adults and young people in the evaluation schools. (Sebba and Robinson, 2010: 3)

The evidence seems very clear that schools which focus on the United Nations Convention on the Rights of the Child, in a structured, systematic and supported way, begin to help children understand the advantages of living in a community. There are four key areas of impact for children at a Rights Respecting School: well-being, participation, relationships and self-esteem. The difference that a Rights Respecting School makes goes beyond the school gates, making a positive impact on the whole community.[1]

Resource 6B(ii) is a summary of the UN Convention for you to use in your school.[2] Print this out and annotate it at one of your leadership meetings. Pin it up in the staffroom and invite comment. Any school that is able to anchor its work to this document will develop real moral strength. Resource 6B(iii) could be placed alongside the summary document to encourage staff to respond to it.

By promoting the values of respect, dignity and non-discrimination, children's self-esteem and well-being is boosted and they are less likely to suffer from stress. A child who understands their own rights also understands how they and others should be treated, and their sense of self-worth is strengthened. The RRSA provides a model of involvement in the creation of a school culture that creates thinking, enquiring and challenging citizens who are purposefully engaged in thinking about the nature of the community in which they live and who are participants in the advancement of that community.

Key questions

Do your students really understand what it means to be a citizen rather than a subject or a slave?

To what extent are your school values actively debated, both in principle and practice?

---

1   For more on Rights Respecting Schools see: https://www.unicef.org.uk/rights-respecting-schools/.
2   The summary can also be found at: https://www.unicef.org.uk/wp-content/uploads/2010/05/UNCRC_summary-1.pdf.

What opportunities do pupils have to act as citizens in the school community?

How confident are staff in embedding debate about values into all subject areas and supporting a critical perspective?

Resources (Download)

6B(i)   Evaluating the progress of citizenship in your school
6B(ii)   A summary of the UN Convention on the Rights of the Child
6B(iii) Accompanying grid for the summary UN Convention on the Rights of the Child

6C

C   Education for sustainability

Why is this an important topic for conversation?

It seems melodramatic to discuss the future of humanity, and yet on current estimates some aspects of climate change will have negative effects on the planet as we know it within the next few decades. If we think in terms of 30 years hence, then this year's primary school leavers will be 41 and secondary school leavers will be 48 – barely middle aged but by certain criteria already living in a very different world.

Should we be educating young people to thrive in a world that could be potentially transformed, or a world that is an extension of the one in which we have lived our lives? Should we be teaching them skills and helping them to develop attitudes which could help to make the planet of the future a more habitable home than some scientists currently predict?

Key quotes for the section

> It is almost certainly too late to stop or reverse climate change ... On the other hand, slowing climate change would be a very important goal, one that would bring huge benefits to the global poor and to future generations.
>
> **(Singer, 2015: 145)**

> Contemporary lifeways for human beings are hardly anything like their lifeways of 100,000 or even 500 years ago. The average use by each human and his or her activities (including electricity, heating and goods that required energy for their manufacture) is several orders of magnitude higher than the energy share of our human ancestors, an attainment that comes with a dark side: our huge and precarious impact on the environment.
>
> **(Perkins, 2014: 9)**

Section discussion

Small nation states like the Maldives and Vanuatu are very far from Europe, in every sense, but in many ways they represent in microcosm the future challenges facing many countries. For the people of these islands climate change is a grim reality that has a real and current impact – it is not a hypothetical or contentious future possibility but a reality that grows in significance every year.

For the Maldives, Vanuatu and other small island developing states climate change is the most significant single threat to sustainable development. One direct consequence of global warming is the increase in extreme weather events. Rising ocean temperatures and ocean acidification will also have a big impact on marine fisheries, significantly affecting the distribution, species mix and productivity of fish stocks. Other impacts that small island states are already experiencing include rising sea levels, coastal erosion and vulnerability to natural disasters.

There is much talk of education for the 21st century or education as preparation for life in the future, and on both those premises education should also be about sustainability in the context of climate change. There is a great deal of activity across educational institutions designed to raise awareness of the issues involved in man-made global warming and the practical measures necessary to change our habits. While these may feel positive many actually have little to no impact. Switching off lights, capturing rainwater and recycling are worthy acts but may make negligible difference. MacAskill (2015: 168) highlights the following issues:

→ Leaving your TV on standby each night over the course of a whole year contributes less to your carbon footprint than driving your car for just two hours.

→ Turning lights off has marginal impact as lighting accounts for only 3% of domestic energy use.

→ Stopping using plastic bags would save only 0.4% of your total emissions.

→ Using locally sourced food is overhyped as only 10% of the carbon footprint for food comes from transportation – 80% comes from production.

MacAskill makes the point that 'The most effective ways to cut down your emissions are to reduce your intake of meat (especially beef), and to reduce the amount you travel' (ibid.: 160).

Resource 6C(i) is a bubble diagram for use with pupils, staff and leaders to consider what effect(s) (both positive and negative) the school might be having on the environment.

Given the politicisation of environmental issues, there are sensitivities about the stance that schools could take. At the same time, there is enough valid science for schools to be confident in three important respects: (1) addressing the issue of climate change through the curriculum, (2) encouraging and supporting meaningful and appropriate actions at both school and community level, and (3) the use of technology to research and communicate on a worldwide level.

Encourage your leadership team to evaluate current progress and develop priorities for next steps, perhaps using the following list as a starting point. Resource 6C(ii) presents this list in table form.

→ Teach children about the 3 R's: reduce waste, reuse resources and recycle materials.

→ Explain why trees are important to the environment. Organise tree planting days in the school and across the community.

→ Encourage children to switch off all appliances and lights when not in use.

→ Move from paper to digital communication as soon as possible.

→ Ensure taps are closed properly after you have used them and use water sparingly.

→ Use materials from the UNESCO-UNEP International Environmental Education Programme.

→ Encourage school based research on environmental issues.

→ Devote one week a year to collaborative environmentally themed projects.

→ Adopt an environmental charity.

→ Ensure that school meals are ecologically sensitive (i.e. recognise the importance of food provenance and manufacturing practices).

→ Promote walking, cycling and scootering to school.

→ Establish links with schools in more environmentally fragile regions of the world.

→ Become an Eco-School (www.eco-schools.org.uk).

→ When the opportunity arises ensure that any new building work incorporates materials and technologies which reduce environmental impact.

Perhaps the most important contribution a school can make to education for sustainability is to embody one of the key themes of environmental awareness: mutual shared responsibility and collective action. Schools working together with community organisations on projects that demonstrate collective responsibility for the environment are far more powerful than polemic or indignation, however well justified. Children who are aware of their personal carbon footprint and have an awareness of their impact on fragile environments are far more likely to be amenable to exploring changes in their behaviour.

The environmentally sensitive school will turn off lights and stop dripping taps, but it will also consider not serving meat, not flying off on excursions around the globe and working to ensure that the majority of members of the school community walk or use public transport to get to work.

Key questions

How aware are you as a leadership team of the issues surrounding climate change?

Is there a school strategy to support sustainability?

Does your curriculum reflect the importance of environmental issues?

As a school, or as part of a multi-academy trust, do you have a shared approach to working across the community to enhance sustainability?

Resources (Download)

6C(i) How does your school impact the environment?

6C(ii) Evaluating your school's positive contribution to sustainability and detailing next steps

D   Respect – demanded or given?

Why is this an important topic for conversation?

'These kids just don't have any respect' is an often heard cry from frustrated teachers. However, a few yards away in another classroom there will be a group of young people clearly demonstrating respect towards a colleague. Maybe there was a time when pupils arrived at the school gate full of admiration for the person about to educate them, just because the adult was 'more educated' than they were. However, one must be wary of rose-tinted spectacles, forgetting the actuality of the classroom – we must make sure we are not confusing fear with respect. We have heard many a tale from our grandparents' time about things that happened when the teacher's back was turned!

The key aspect of this topic can be emphasised by considering an extreme case: 'Is a pupil who has no respect at all for the person in front of them likely to benefit educationally?' Given that the answer is clearly no, the follow-up question must be: 'Can respect be nurtured?'

Key quotes for the section

> For pupils in general the most important attributes of good teachers are that they should be 'human', should be able to 'teach' and make you 'work', and keep control. They should also 'respect' pupils if they wish the respect to be returned. This respect has to be earned – it is not an automatic right. Some teachers are felt to be inhuman. They interpret their role too literally.
>
> **(Woods, 1990: 14)**

> Respect lasts you a lifetime. It's morals. It's manners. It's about coaching students to feel good enough about themselves – because a better you starts with a respectful you. It means showing everyone respect, including yourself. [...] Respect is at the heart of cutting down on exclusions in schools. [...] Teach respect, don't simply expect it. Model it. Live it.
>
> **(Roberson, 2012: 34–36)**

> The value of respect in school cannot be undersold. [...] A lack of respect can be downright detrimental, completely undermining the mission of teaching and learning. In recent years, it seems that a 'respectful learning environment' is almost non-existent in many schools across the country.
>
> **(Meader, 2016)**

> Respect is a two-way street – if you want to get it, you've got to give it.
>
> **(Anon.)**

> I speak to everyone in the same way, whether he is the garbage man or the president of the university.
>
> **(attributed to Albert Einstein)**

Section discussion

It is simply untrue to suggest that the 'youth of today' have no respect – certain groups even greet each other with a fist bump and a call of 'respect'. What is clear is that they don't necessarily have an inherent respect for teachers! As described in the quotes above, respect seems to be a value which is most evident when it is first given rather than simply expected.

Respect can be considered from three perspectives: the school's demonstrated respect for pupils, how teachers show respect for the pupils and, finally, how pupils demonstrate respect for the school and its staff.

School's respect for pupils

A first step for any school might be to consider the respect that the school and staff exhibit for the pupils in their care. Resource 6D(i) is designed to begin considering the question from the pupils' perspective by breaking down the school day into sections including arrival at school, movement in school, relationship with teachers, breaks and lunches, and even the experience of using the toilet! Some school leaders may be surprised, or even annoyed, to be given such a challenging list. 'We aren't running a hotel' or 'Do you think money grows on trees?' are both responses that may be heard.

(There are a couple of high profile ex-inspectors who relate that they could often tell how good a school was going to be by walking into the pupils' toilets – great schools would have toilets that demonstrated a respect for the pupils in their care.)

If the areas on the list are considered honestly it will give the school leader an overview of the innate respect the school demonstrates for its pupils. The more positive the response given, the stronger the respect. Therefore, if you accept that it is important to demonstrate trust towards students, using time and resources to improve the physical environment of the school is not a distraction to the main work of the school but central to its development.

Teachers' respect for pupils

This is a difficult one – the hackles will already be rising for some readers! For some this is a fundamental issue: they feel that their role as a teacher should mean they are respected and it is not their job to be the one first demonstrating respect. However, think of a teacher you know who is respected by many pupils. What characteristics do you observe? It is quite likely that they treat pupils with respect. As Jim Roberson says, 'Teach respect, don't simply expect it!' The teachers who are most respected by pupils are those who, in turn, treat them with most respect. This does not mean that the teacher is 'easy' and pupils always get their way – that is not respect, that is capitulation!

The respectful teacher will sometimes deliver some very strong messages, but they do so in a way that makes it clear that they have a high regard for the pupils in front of them. When an issue needs to be addressed it is couched in language such as, 'This is your choice – are you really happy that this is the best you can do?' Whenever possible young people are encouraged to respect themselves. A pupil who is intrinsically motivated, rather than needing constant 'nagging' by the teacher, is more likely to succeed.

Many children who are seriously unhappy with their school life report that they feel distant to the process of education and that they feel 'done to'. Co-construction of learning and planning of future work in collaboration with pupils demonstrates the teacher's respect for their individuality.

Pupils' respect for teachers

How would you rate the current levels of respect shown by your pupils towards their teachers? Use resource 6D(ii) to gather your thoughts. As a leadership team, observe the way the pupils interact with the school and its teachers. Observe them arriving at the school, during breaktimes and lunchtimes, and the way they interact with each other and, more importantly, any staff members that pass by. Observe lessons, focusing on the interactions between pupils and teacher. For the final section of the resource, follow a few pupils and watch the levels of respect they demonstrate with different teachers. Try to identify the characteristics of the teachers who engender either respect or disrespect. When the leadership team have each completed this task, focus your conversation on how levels of trust in the school can be further developed.

Clearly, telling pupils that they need to respect their teachers and school is unlikely to be effective on its own. The school needs to be a place where respect is demonstrated by all: by leaders to teachers, by teachers to teachers, by teachers to parents and so on. If respect is the common language and attitude within the school, then it is more likely that the pupils will give teachers the respect they deserve.

Key questions

Is your school a place of respect?

Does your school building show respect to the pupils?

Does the school day show respect for the pupils?

Do teachers demonstrate respect to all pupils?

Do the pupils show respect for their teachers and the school?

Resources (Download)

6D(i) How much do you respect the pupils in your school?

6D(ii) Analysing how your pupils respect their teachers

6E

E   Student leadership

Why is this an important topic for conversation?

If education is about more than subject based academic success, then it has to be focused on the social dimensions of the lives that students will lead – and for many reasons that includes experience of leading and being led.

There is increasing recognition that leadership is not about the power and status of the few but, rather, is best understood as the collective capacity of the school – that is, leadership is a resource to which all can contribute. The most significant outcomes of education are often directly related to the quality of leadership; just as adults need to be effective learners, so students need to be effective leaders.

Key quotes for the section

> Any school that has to impose the teaching of democracy is already suspect. The less democratic schools are, the more they need to teach about democratic ideals. If schools were really democratic, in the sense of providing opportunities for children to experience democracy through practice, they wouldn't feel the need to indoctrinate them with platitudes about democracy.
>
> **(Chomsky, 2000: 27)**

> Students are usually the targets of change efforts and services. Rarely are they change partners. Students are highly knowledgeable about the things that help them learn – teachers who know their material, care for them, have a sense of humour and never give up on them, for example. Finnish schools work very well because children are expected to be responsible from an early age. [...] Students can also be involved in changing their peers, often in ways that are as powerful as those that are used by their teachers.
>
> **(Hargreaves and Shirley, 2009: 83)**

Section discussion

There are three broad justifications for moving beyond pupil voice towards student leadership. First, an organisation or community can never have too much leadership; the central concept is 'total leadership' or 'leadership in depth'. Second, it is important to move from the theory of spiritual, moral, social and cultural development (SMSC) to the reality of practical service to the school and wider community, and that necessarily involves leadership. Third, involvement in leadership is a potentially powerful source of personal development.

Before reading further, use resource 6E(i) to identify examples of student leadership already existing in your school. For each area, identify how many pupils are involved and what age they are. Rate the quality of your current work in this area.

The language of student leadership has traditionally involved roles such as head boy and head girl, form captains and, most commonly, prefects. The traditional role of prefects has been focused largely on providing a positive role model and supporting teachers in the day-to-day running of the school, notably managing breaktimes and lunchtimes. There seems little doubt that these roles have benefits for both school and individual – in particular, it is a useful endorsement of maturity, responsibility and engagement for future employers.

Staricoff (2013: 29) describes the development of pupil leadership in an infant school:

> *This year, we have started work on involving the children in the SDP [school development plan], so we have elected learning leaders from each class who will create a child version of the school's SDP. [...] It will be written in their own language.*

Leadership is thus shared rather than distributed and is contingent on context. In this respect, the school as a community offers a very powerful opportunity for citizenship education in practice, with real choices and responsibilities available for pupils. As in the example from Hertford Infant and Nursery School described above, the most obvious area for pupil leadership is in learning, but there are also opportunities in terms of managing the school site and developing relationships across the wider community, not least with other schools. Possible opportunities for student leadership might include:

→ Managing a key budget.

→ Acting as learning mentors, working through peer coaching and peer assessment.

→ Play leaders initiating positive play habits and devising new games.

→ Reading buddies.

→ Leading sports teams and sports coaching.

→ Leading special projects such as charity events and developing links across the community.

→ Having responsibility for an area of the school grounds in terms of resources, planting and management.

→ Running services for other pupils (e.g. a healthy eating tuck shop).

Resource 6E(ii) presents the above information in a tabular form for you to consider ways to improve student leadership at your school.

The crucial issue here is that students have genuine authority to act, which in turn means having the ability to exercise real choices, within a budget if appropriate.

A more radical example that is well tried and tested in many independent schools is to move away from the traditional year based lateral structure of the school into what might be described as a family based structure. For example, pupils might be organised into families of six to eight members, with a representative from each year group, so the main social experience of the school would be that of a (large by modern standards) group of siblings. Senior students have significant pastoral responsibility for the well-being of their group, with appropriate support and guidance.

Another possible area, building on the example provided by Staricoff, is the active involvement of students in the leadership and management of the school. This moves the school council beyond uniforms and the lunch menu into the core business of teaching and learning. This is obviously a sensitive area, but given the emphasis in the Ofsted framework (2016) on listening to pupils' experience during inspections, it might be a significant step towards authentic inclusion. Possible areas of activity might include aspects of choice across the curriculum, the learner experience and reflecting the experience of childhood in the 21st century.

Underpinning all of these possible areas is the need for a leadership development programme for pupils that provides training in the skills and strategies appropriate to their role, such as:

→ Learning to engage with change.

→ Working collaboratively in meetings and on projects.

→ Time and project management, task completion.

→ Thinking skills – analysing, synthesising and developing coherent and logical arguments.

→ Building consensus, negotiating and securing commitment.

These skills relate very strongly to ideas about education for life and employability. They are also essential components of active citizenship and personal confidence in social situations. What is educationally important is that student leadership leads to key educational outcomes, which may include:

→ Real, purposeful and socially useful activities with valid and significant outcomes.

→ Personal challenge that leads to increased confidence and growth.

→ Personal management such as planning and reviewing progress.

→ Reflection on personal development and growth.

A useful approach might be to turn the whole question on its head and try to identify the skills that you want your pupils to develop in school. From this list, identify those that could be advanced by developing your pupil leadership. Remember: true leadership is possible from the very young, not just the 'grown-ups'.

Key questions

How effectively is leadership distributed across the school?

What opportunities are there for students to learn through social service?

Does the school's SMSC include provision for leadership development?

How authentic and significant is student voice? Would your students agree?

Resources (Download)

6E(i)   What is the current status of pupil leadership in your school?
6E(ii)   Developing the pupil leadership in your school

Alternative staffing models

A   Recruiting and retaining staff

Why is this an important topic for conversation?

Whenever there is a shift in society's priorities, there always follows a change in the supply and demand of sectors of the workforce, and this is particularly true in teaching. Around the world at the moment the situation is very diverse: in some countries there are more qualified teachers than vacancies for them to fill, while in others there is a general shortage of trained teachers. Besides this macro variation, there are also specific shortages in almost every country – in one country it may be science teachers and in another maths, and as new subjects are developed people are required to teach them. There can be as much as a 10 year gap between identifying a deficit in a particular area and solving that problem. Once the politicians agree that there is a problem, it may take a few years to come up with a solution and a further few years to develop capacity in training and then develop interest in it. So, for many school leaders a real priority for them is to attract quality staff to join their team and then to keep them.

Key quotes for the section

> The fact that teachers can vary in effectiveness [...] raises an important issue regarding the value of particular policies in promoting recruitment or retention. One cannot assume that an improvement in recruitment or retention rates is, per se, a valuable outcome. If these improvements are achieved at the expense of quality, then students may experience more harm than benefit from such a policy.
>
> **(Guarino et al., 2006: 176–177)**

7A

> The research provides strong support for the conclusion that compensation plays a key role in the recruitment and retention of teachers. Not surprisingly, the research indicates that increasing compensation tends to increase the rate of teacher retention, but this relationship is not a simple one. Compensation has a varying impact on retention depending on other factors such as teachers' gender, level of experience and current job satisfaction.
>
> **(Allen, 2005: ix)**

> Teacher turnover can also undermine schools' efforts to implement reforms; successful school reform requires sustained and shared commitment by school staff. Staff turnover means that new teachers, unfamiliar with and uncommitted to these reforms, must somehow be brought on board.
>
> **(Scherer, 2003: 5)**

Section discussion

There are many reasons why teacher recruitment and retention is a key issue for a majority of leadership teams around the world. At the most simplistic level, without sufficient teachers in a school there will be logistical issues in ensuring that all pupils have a high quality learning experience. On a financial level, advertising and recruiting for new teachers is a costly business and in many countries this cost is borne directly by the school, causing the school to make a choice between spending its budget on pupil resources or staff recruitment. On a human level, the disruption to pupils' relationships and to planned initiatives within the school can be severe. However, as the Guarino et al. quote eloquently describes, low turnover of staff is not necessarily the perfect situation. Some school leaders will use an annual figure of around 20% turnover as an ideal. For many this is a luxury they are not afforded, as some schools (particularly those in challenging areas) can experience turnover rates at the other extreme (20% retention and 80% churn).

Some school leaders will immediately turn to this section to find the answer to their recruitment problems. The sad fact is that there is no magic wand, only ideas that have worked for certain schools. Each of the approaches that follow have worked for some but, regrettably, they may not work for your school. Below we set out the advantages and disadvantages of each strategy.

Training/coaching programmes

Some schools use the fact that they have detailed and intensive training/coaching systems to recruit new staff. Training is often linked to national teaching standards for that country and will include a mix of internal and external trainers. At its most effective it will involve teachers of all levels in the school, not just the new ones. It should also be backed up by a coaching system whereby teachers with compatible styles work collaboratively. Some of these programmes may also be linked to a master's programme, enabling teachers to develop their career; for some of the most professional teachers this will serve as a magnet for your school.

Downside: expensive in resources and time; important to deliver real outcomes to staff; the pairings of some staff can be problematic; overcrowding of a busy week.

Grow your own programmes

In some parts of the world the solution to the recruitment headache has been to allow schools to invest money in developing programmes to train their own staff. Some schools target university graduates from non-teacher training courses straight from college and offer them a training programme that results in them gaining qualified teacher status. This can produce a team of highly loyal and motivated staff who understand the particular needs and issues faced by the pupils of your school.

Downside: this is very expensive and requires a large commitment of time and money; in the early days of training it is possible that the quality of teaching might be below par; some trainee teachers will inevitably not make the grade and this is lost investment.

Enhanced salary/golden handshake

Some of the long term research projects in this field (e.g. the Michael Allen report quoted on page 138) highlight this as an area where some of the strongest positive effects on recruitment can be found. In other words, spending money on increasing teachers' financial rewards is effective. Sometimes this is in the form of a permanent or limited time increase in salary, in others it is in the form of a one-off golden handshake (a single payment made to candidates with a required skill/subject expertise).

Downside: this may create issues with your current staff, either increasing their dissatisfaction or causing knock-on increases in their salaries; the effect may push people to do the job for the money rather than for the pupils; these teachers are in area of need (a need shared by most other schools) so keeping these teachers once you have trained them may be difficult.

Housing

Some schools have found that letting flats or houses to prospective employees has been a very successful strategy. This is particularly useful in city areas. Schools report a marked interest from candidates and that the initial introduction to the school has been smoother because of it.

Downside: the set-up of this depends on either having some housing stock attached to the school or the ability to source good quality housing stock; many school leaders do not relish the idea of being de facto landlords; this may not prove to be a long term solution; the availability of housing may not always match the recruitment needs.

Computing equipment

Some schools have purchased a variety of technology for their staff, which they then advertise as a benefit of the job. This offer seems particularly popular with younger teachers coming straight from college. It also ensures that all teachers have the latest compatible technology and sends a message that the school is one where ICT literacy is expected among its staff.

Downside: this can be very expensive initially and once started it may be necessary to maintain and upgrade the computers; in an increasingly connected world many prospective candidates may already have the technology you offer (or even better).

Guaranteeing maximum contact hours and no cover

Some schools try to guarantee an enhanced work–life balance by restricting the number of contact hours. Some employ a bank of 'cover teachers' who ensure that in the case of absent colleagues no teaching staff are expected to cover the lesson, therefore guaranteeing their non-contact time.

Downside: this is expensive and can create difficulties in times of high teacher absence; making effective use of a central 'cover team' can be problematic.

Appointment to a group of schools

Where schools are encouraged to work together, appointing together can have a number of benefits. Sometimes the collective power of the schools is more attractive to prospective candidates: the idea that a young teacher can try out more than one type of school (maybe even different age groups) while still having a guaranteed job can be appealing. By collaborating it may be more feasible to offer some of the other attractions described above.

Downside: some candidates may be put off by not having their own base; if recruitment is approached across a group of schools the number of vacancies (and adverts) will increase, potentially giving the appearance of turmoil; spreading costs and issuing contracts can be problematic.

Buying into the ethos

Some schools report that some of their most successful long term recruitment drives have been achieved when they emphasise the journey the school is on – the reason the school exists and its values and ethos. Done badly this can come across as insincere and may put off prospective candidates. However, some schools have had success with taking a more personal approach and ensuring that applicants 'feel' the ethos of the school. Making your advert stand out from others is always difficult, but it is often worth the effort.

Downside: this is very time consuming and it is possible to have the opposite effect, and not appear sincere at all.

Use resource 7A(i) to promote discussion among your team. Use the priority column to decide which of the solutions might work best for your school. If retention is your concern, 7A(ii) can be used to address this problem. The solutions are much the same but the effectiveness in your school may well be different to those for recruitment.

If strategies for either recruitment or retention prove unsuccessful, it may be worth looking at the problem from a different perspective. Are there ways to reimagine the teaching in your school? Section 7C may help.

Key questions

What is your priority – recruitment or retention?

What do you currently do? How effective is each strategy?

What other strategies could you consider?

How could they be adapted to work in your school?

Do you need to reframe the problem and change what you do?

Resources (Download)

7A(i)   Looking at the solutions for recruitment in your school

7A(ii)   Looking at the solutions for retention in your school

B   Professionalising volunteering

Why is this an important topic for conversation?

Teachers do not have a monopoly on knowledge. Equally, learning is not defined by time in school or academic subjects. It is really important to bring as many different voices as possible into schools in order to enhance provision and enrich learning experiences and opportunities. At a time of economic stringency, volunteers can make crucial contributions to the life of the school.

Key quote for the section

> Three broad approaches to volunteering can be identified, not for profit, civil society and 'serious leisure':
>
> ... not for profit – From this perspective, opportunities for volunteering are provided by large professionally staffed and formally structured organisations. While these are most likely to be charities or third sector organisations, they also include statutory agencies such as hospitals and schools. Volunteers provide them with a significant additional resource in the form of unpaid labour and are increasingly treated as 'human resources' which need formal and skilled management ...
>
> ... civil society – [T]heir involvement in social welfare is less likely to be focused on delivering care and other services than in offering mutual support in self-help groups or campaigning for improvements in provision.
>
> ... serious leisure might, for example, involve participation in the organisation of a sporting or cultural event. Examples might include theatre, music and dance.
>
> **(Rochester et al., 2012: 11–13)**

Section discussion

To begin with, it is worth stressing that volunteers are not amateurs. For example, virtually every aspect of the RNLI's work is done by volunteers and yet it is difficult to imagine a more effective organisation or one that makes a greater impact. Nor are volunteers only deployed in lower order tasks. Perhaps the largest group of volunteers in schools are governors and trustees, and their strategic role requires highly professional knowledge and skills. So, to a very real extent the education system is overseen by volunteers. Similarly, most museums and stately homes would not remain open without the help of volunteers.

Volunteering is a key indicator of a successful community. Volunteers provide a service with an altruistic or philanthropic intention, and this is a significant marker of a morally healthy society. Equally, volunteering provides opportunities for self-help, mutual aid and working interdependently – all powerful indicators of high social capital and effective communities. The potential benefits of volunteering for schools might be listed as:

→ Providing a more diverse range of skills, experience and knowledge.

→ Helping to ensure consistently high quality learning experiences for more pupils.

→ Raising awareness about your school across the community.

→ Building relationships within the community that your school serves and contributing to supporting others in your community. Volunteering provides opportunities for social inclusion, skills development and potential routes to employment.

→ There is evidence that volunteering can help to improve people's health and well-being. Older people, in particular, can gain significant physical and psychological benefits from involvement with others, and long term engagement is likely to be far more valuable than the annual Christmas lunch and carol concert.

→ Volunteers with significant professional expertise can support the development and delivery of school services and specific projects by bringing in new opinions, ideas and approaches. This can help you to adapt and stay relevant to what your school and pupils need, as well as identify opportunities to improve and refine services.

→ When effective and efficient (and not to the detriment of employees), the support provided by volunteers can help to save money and resources.

Possible opportunities for recruiting and involving volunteers include:

→ Acting as reading buddies.

→ Becoming a member of the 'granny cloud' – people who volunteer to talk to, read with, question and encourage schoolchildren via Skype (see Mitra, 2014).

→ Sitting and talking with the children at lunchtime.

→ Supporting aspiration in careers talks.

→ Providing expertise in gardening or running an allotment.

→ Bringing animals into the school.

→ Advising on technical issues in ICT, building and other projects.

→ Developing resources such as displays of student work.

→ Supporting school concerts and productions.

→ Advising on management procedures (e.g. risk assessment, due diligence).

→ Providing 'living history' talks.

→ Advising on ethnicity issues.

→ Building relationships with local public services, notably the police and fire services.

Recruiting volunteers for schools obviously has to be done in the context of a Disclosure and Barring Service (DBS) check and based on an understanding of the principles and practice of safeguarding and risk assessment. As well as these formal requirements, volunteers need to be aware of their duty to observe strict confidentiality and not pass opinion on sensitive matters outside the school. It is also very important that volunteers do not compromise their position by dealing with issues affecting their own children. They also need to avoid having favourites and discourage the children from becoming dependent on them – pupils should always be urged to try things for themselves. It is obviously important for volunteers to follow the school's dress code. Finally, it is vital that children are not lifted, carried or moved in any way.

These guidelines can be personalised and issued to any volunteer before they begin work using resource 7B(i).

The volunteer involvement ideas listed above are produced in table form in resource 7B(ii). Use this to develop the areas of volunteering in your school, identifying ways each method might be used and then highlighting priorities.

Many people seek out voluntary opportunities because they don't want to be employees. They enjoy the engagement and motivation, as well as the sense of public service and moral commitment, but not the control and bureaucracy. It is therefore inappropriate to have job descriptions, performance indicators and the usual plethora of HR bureaucracy for volunteers; however, there is a need for a shared understanding of mutual expectations and obligations. In large schools and multi-academy trusts (MATs) it may well be appropriate to appoint a volunteer coordinator (themselves a volunteer) who works to ensure optimum mutual benefit.

Trust has the potential to develop a sense of extended community and engagement which really makes a difference in how successful volunteering works. The willingness to volunteer is a direct corollary of the extent of authentic trust and mutual advantage.

Key questions

Do you actively seek to recruit volunteers?

Are volunteers treated with the necessary respect?

Do you provide appropriate support and resources to enhance the contribution of volunteers?

Have you audited where volunteers could make a significant difference in your school?

Have you considered developing a directory of volunteers across your community?

Resources (Download)

    7B(i)   Guidelines for volunteering in your school

    7B(ii)   Possible volunteering opportunities for your school

C   Structure vs. flexibility

Why is this an important topic for conversation?

As we all know, the world is changing at an unprecedented rate. The challenges for young people today are very different to those of our own generation. Schools are facing demands and restrictions unimaginable 30 years ago and are being scrutinised with many of the tools used in business. It would be ridiculous to suggest that a school's response to all this change should be to remain unchanged itself. The perfect school for a 1950s world is not going to provide all the answers for one in 2020. If we agree with these statements, then it is illogical to assume that the staffing structures of the past are fit for the future. In times of rapid transformation, it seems likely that we should be aiming for a more flexible approach to staffing.

Key quotes for the section

> Organizational structure is the skeletal framework within which people carry out their work. Structure can enhance or hinder individual performance and the accomplishment of school goals. Effective educational leaders direct structural changes that will establish positive conditions for teaching and learning.
>
> **(Leithwood and Riehl, 2003: 5)**

> Organizational coherence on basic aims and values, then, is a precondition for the exercise of any effective leadership around instructional improvement. Collaboration and collegiality among teachers, and among head teachers and principals, is a necessary but not sufficient condition for improvement. Distributed leadership poses the challenge of how to distribute responsibility and authority for guidance and direction of instruction, and learning about instruction, so as to increase the likelihood that the decisions of individual teachers and principals about what to do, and what to learn how to do, aggregate into collective benefits for student learning.
>
> **(Elmore, 2000: 17–18)**

> Effective school leadership [...] entails the promotion of cooperation rather than competition, the development of joy in work and fulfilment in learning and the driving out of all forms of fear. School leadership must involve helping people to do a better job, in a happier work like atmosphere, for their own benefit and for the benefit of the whole school, its children, its parents and its community.
>
> **(INTO, 1996: 30)**

> You must always be able to predict what's next and then have the flexibility to evolve.
>
> **(Marc Benioff, quoted in Harris, 2009)**

Section discussion

A simplistic description of a typical model of schooling from 100 years ago would be: a school board appoints a teacher and then the teacher teaches the children a set curriculum. As schools became bigger this evolved into: the education department appoints a head teacher, who then appoints teaching staff, who then teach the pupils a curriculum agreed by the head teacher. In many areas of the world this then evolved into a more complex pyramid arrangement, with government at the top and layers of local councils, governing bodies and then a head teacher who, in turn, subdivides their work via a series of deputies and specific task-orientated roles. In some secondary schools the staffing structure has evolved into a gigantic flow chart (often shaped like a pyramid) with a dazzling array of interconnections and role titles. The key word here is *evolved*. The changes in structure have been driven by the changing world. As new priorities emerge, the usual demand is, 'We need schools to play their part in helping the pupils to prepare for this.' This has caused a subsequent knee-jerk response from school leaders: 'We need someone to lead this.' This has resulted in a plethora of new jobs, from head of computing through to coordinator of avoiding radicalism and parenting skills leader. Each new problem seems to require a new position.

This 'sticking plaster' approach to staffing has resulted in school structures that have become incredibly complex and often impractical. Historical decisions have been made because person A was the right person for the job, which they then took on alongside their existing role. These two roles then become linked together – so when person A leaves, the school looks for a suitable person to fill their shoes. In addition, most countries have detailed rules and regulations in place to protect the working conditions of employees, so it is easy to understand why many schools choose not to change their internal structure even though it may have existed for many years. In times of economic abundance, when countries have sufficient capital to lavish on education, it is possible to prop up a traditional system simply by adding more roles and by increasing salaries. However, in times of austerity the demand is to do more for less.

Few (if any) schools can honestly say they have a completely efficient staffing structure – one where all the needs of the school and its pupils are met efficiently and quickly by the people in the organisation best suited to fulfil that role. Accepting that this is an issue for your school may be challenging, as the turmoil caused and work created by any significant change is likely to be considerable. However, while it may be tempting to sweep structural change under the carpet, we would not recommend this as a long term strategy.

Instead, the brave leadership team can have an honest look at the school's current staffing structure using resource 7C(i). This task must be carried out in as impersonal a way as possible – the review should not be about the individuals but about the roles they are being asked to perform. Inevitably, some of the people carrying out the analysis will be trying to consider their own role in a 'removed' way. For this reason, the task should be undertaken by both internal and external personnel to try to obtain as broad and honest a picture as possible.

Once complete, the next stage would be to consider the roles you actually need at this moment and the roles you think you will need in the future. Resource 7C(ii) is intended to support this exercise. Try to move away from defining very specific leadership roles – these by their nature have short termism at their heart. Try to identify roles which are clear but have a broader application – ones that can add and drop initiatives as required. Make them about the aspirations of the role and what the job actually involves. Where possible, think of the roles you require as a team and how they link together, rather than designing a tree of who is in charge of whom. Use the ideas in resource 7C(iii) to consider different ways to present this information. Experiment with how the roles could be depicted, and how they interact both with each other and with the core aims of the school. Remember, this may not be achievable in one step (or without significant angst!). However, by adopting a new approach any shifts in staffing can be used to move towards the new goal, rather than to simply replicate what has always been.

Be imaginative. Few of us expect the world to become less challenging or to revert to an age gone by. New ways of leading are needed for this new world, and there seems little doubt that flexibility and adaptability are essential.

Key questions

Is your current staffing structure efficient and effective?

Do some of the roles you have exist purely for historical reasons?

What do you really need from your staffing structures over the coming years?

How could you reimagine your structure to match this?

What shape would best illustrate the staffing structure your school needs?

Resources (Download)

7C(i)	Looking at the staffing structure in your school
7C(ii)	What do you need from your staffing structure?
7C(iii)	Non-pyramid approaches to staffing structures

D   All staff as a leader

Why is this an important topic for conversation?

There is a clear and well-established causal relationship between effective leadership and school improvement. There is usually a strong emphasis on the role of the principal or head teacher as the determining factor, whereas in fact it would be more appropriate to consider the overall leadership capacity of the school. Even in a small primary school, let alone a large secondary, leadership is too complex, too demanding and too high stakes to reside with just one person.

Key quotes for the section

> [Definitions often tend] to regard leadership as a noun rather than a verb, *something* that leaders possess rather than *a process* in which they are participants. [...] [L]eader-centricity tends to obscure, if not completely overlook, the role that *followers* play.
>
> **(Haslam et al., 2011: 17; original emphasis)**

> The key notion in this definition is that leadership is about learning together, and constructing meaning and knowledge collectively and collaboratively. It involves opportunities to surface and mediate perceptions, values, beliefs, information, and assumptions through continuing conversations [and] to inquire about and generate ideas together.
>
> **(Lambert, 1998: 5–6)**

Section discussion

The central challenge of this section is to see leadership as collective capacity rather than personal status; in other words, moving away from the focus on the individual and looking instead at leadership as a collective potential to be realised. This involves a range of strategies and changes in culture. This is not to argue for a utopian model of participation in which the moot or something similar is given the final voice. Leadership decisions are so complex and have such significant potential outcomes that those who are affected by them should be aware of the changes and have an appropriate level of involvement.

The crucial change in terms of culture is the move away from a top down, permission seeking, permission giving culture – and this, of course, is directly related to the level of trust in the organisation and the quality of working relationships. In this context, trust is best understood as a balancing act between authority and responsibility. In traditional hierarchies leaders allocate responsibilities with varying degrees of authority, thus influencing and controlling teachers' ability to act. In many organisations the balance of responsibility and authority is expressed most directly in terms of promotion up the career ladder – increasing responsibility with increasing authority.

Distributed leadership could not be more different. Levels of responsibility are seen in terms of technical complexity rather than personal ability, and it is assumed that teachers and others will have a level of authority appropriate to their expertise, experience and proven success. Authority is thus associated with ability rather than age or status. The implications for school culture include:

→ Irrespective of role, everyone accepting the need for them to model leadership in their personal sphere of influence, especially with regard to school values and norms.

→ Every individual accepting responsibility for the school as a whole rather than their own part of it.

→ A willingness to act on their own initiative rather than waiting to be asked or told.

→ Accepting personal rather than collective responsibility and accountability when appropriate.

→ Sharing responsibility for developing leadership and building capacity.

→ Encouraging and supporting innovation and helping to lead change.

All staff leading does not mean an end to senior roles, but increasingly the work of heads and deputies is to coordinate and support the leadership of others through coaching, modelling and dialogue.

Coaching provides one of the most significant strategies for leaders to support each other's development. It is usually regarded as more of a short term, authoritative intervention in order to support improved performance or changing strategies and behaviours.

Modelling is concerned with the power of example. Teachers watch what other teachers do in order to check if their actions are consistent over time and to test whether the various leaders do as they say. Teachers do not follow colleagues who cannot 'walk the talk'.

Dialogue is about creating and supporting opportunities for teachers to talk with their colleagues about learning and teaching. The kinds of dialogues that influence what happens in classrooms are focused on teaching and learning. Leaders create the space to meet with colleagues and discuss pedagogy and pupils' learning; however, in the distributed leadership environment teachers are expected to initiate their own dialogues and not seek approval or permission.

Some leaders will report that they use distributed leadership when the reality is somewhat different. One tool to investigate how staff see the school is to utilise a technique used by psychologists called 'the Blob tree'. Resource 7D(i) contains an example, although there are lots of examples on the Internet. Simply ask staff to imagine that the picture depicts the school and to identify which blob represents them and other key colleagues. The actual blob chosen is of less interest than the reasons given for the placement. Do your staff believe they have real leadership?

The practical issues related to shared or distributed leadership include:

→ Changing the language of the school, especially in job descriptions and policies, to recognise leadership as being a collective quality available to all.

→ Ensuring that those staff who wish to are able to contribute to aspects of decision making.

→ Making leadership development available to all members of the school community, including governors, support staff and students.

→ Providing opportunities for all staff to participate in key leadership functions (e.g. rotating membership of certain teams, rotating team roles so everyone has the opportunity to lead the team).

→ Ensuring greater openness and transparency in a range of school policies and procedures (e.g. pupil involvement in development planning and prioritising the budget).

→ Developing mutual accountability and shared performance indicators.

Resource 7D(ii) tabulates the above factors, enabling you to focus your team discussion around how you can increase leadership among the teachers in your school.

Perhaps the best way to understand the implications of distributed leadership is to think of a continuum that ranges from immaturity to maturity: the school will move towards maturity as greater opportunities are afforded for all members of the community to assume the responsibilities of leadership and move away from a dependency culture. One area of challenge will be those staff who are happier, for whatever reason, not accepting leadership responsibility. This is a classic example of the importance of culture change: the consensual basis of the school has to change over time as the early adopters gradually change 'the way things are done around here'. Resource F5(i) from *Leadership Dialogues* is reproduced here as resource 7D(iii) to support your self-reflection in this area.

In leadership context is everything, so it would be nonsense to pretend that challenging the traditional hierarchical structures of education is easy. However, spend time in an early years setting or a special needs classroom and you will see just how possible 'all staff as leaders' is.

Key questions

Would you describe your school as being mature or immature in leadership terms?

What steps are you taking to build leadership capacity and move away from a hierarchical dependency culture?

In what ways is the leadership potential of support staff nurtured and developed?

Do governors see themselves as part of your leadership capacity?

Would you feel it appropriate to add students and parents to your extended leadership capacity?

Resources (Download)

7D(i)   How much leadership responsibility do your staff think they have?

7D(ii)   Developing the conditions for increased staff leadership

7D(iii) How mature/immature is the leadership in your school?

7E

E   Pupils as teachers

Why is this an important topic for conversation?

First, we should make it clear that this is not about the wholesale replacement of teachers by pupils! However, a number of drivers push us towards considering how pupils could carry out some of the roles traditionally carried out by teachers. On a purely financial level, in times of teacher shortage and/or budget tightening, the prospect of spreading some of the teacher's tasks becomes more attractive. Much more importantly, though, there is growing evidence that peer-to-peer teaching can actually enhance that child's learning as well as that of other pupils in the class. A true case of a win-win strategy.

Key quotes for the section

> If students are to develop as learning partners with teachers in a culture of co-construction, then at some point it will become a natural part of the process for students to adopt the role of lead learner or teacher. In many homes, when it comes to the latest computer or piece of technology acquired by the household, the children often take the lead in training the rest of the family in how to use it. If this is the case in homes, why not in schools?
>
> **(Shearer et al., 2007: 25)**

> The outcomes are amazing. Empowered with this level of responsibility, students come up with great ideas for lessons, discover or produce superb resources and demonstrate real authority in leading class discussions. We've refined the process along the way and it can be a bit of a white-knuckle ride at times because you never know exactly what you are going to get.
>
> **(Sherrington, 2012)**

> Peer teaching is not a new concept. It can be traced back to Aristotle's use of *archons*, or student leaders, and to the letters of Seneca the Younger. It was first organized as a theory by Scotsman Andrew Bell in 1795, and later implemented into French and English schools in the 19th century. Over the past 30–40 years, peer teaching has become increasingly popular in conjunction with mixed ability grouping in K-12 public schools and an interest in more financially efficient methods of teaching.
>
> **(Briggs, 2013; original emphasis)**

Section discussion

For over 100 years, the traditional model of schooling has been a group of pupils sitting side by side facing a teacher at the front. The teacher then attempts to transfer the knowledge from inside his head into those of the students before him. This model has endured many changes in society, but this does not mean it is the most effective way to teach. Parents often moan that their child is being uncommunicative when they answer a cheery enquiry of, 'What did you do at school today?' with a shrug of the shoulders and a grunt of, 'Nuffin much/Dunno/Can't remember'. While your child may well be avoiding a longer conversation so they can get on to the important tasks of the day (such as watching TV, playing computer games or checking social media) they may well be telling the truth – they simply can't remember.

It can be quite chastening to carry out a survey with pupils a few hours after a lesson. (Resource 7E(i) is provided to help you do this.) Don't be surprised if the lesson you spent an eternity preparing has quickly faded into the background for many of them. It is interesting to compare your planned (and delivered) variety of activities with what the pupil actually perceives. A lesson may be technically superb, but if the pupils retain little long term information, skills or support from it, we must question its usefulness.

It is important to emphasise that we are not expecting a teacher to walk into a classroom on day one and say, 'Hi, kids – I hear peer teaching is a highly effective strategy. Here is the curriculum – get on with it. I'm in the staffroom if anyone wants me!' We are describing a subtle, collective approach which has the teacher and students discussing the hoped-for outcomes and agreeing the best strategy to get there.

Pupils can play the role of a teacher in a number of ways:

→ *Administrative support*. The pupil carries out administrative functions for the teacher (e.g. completing the register, collating materials). This can be time saving for the teacher and can help with the pupil's self-esteem. However, it has no real positive effect on the pupil's learning and could even distract them from engaging in the intended work.

→ *Report maker.* The pupil (or a group of pupils) makes a report on the work they have completed in the lesson. They treat the remainder of the group as an audience. A refinement of this is that the rest of the group act as advisers and critically review the group's presentation, perhaps giving them pointers on how to improve their work. This has the benefit of consolidating the whole group's learning. It can also be used to introduce new information to the group, although the didactic nature of the inputs may detract from this.

→ *Planning assistant.* The pupil (or a group of pupils) discusses the work to be covered with the teacher and then they jointly plan the best way to deliver it. Some parts of this will be planned and delivered by the pupils themselves using strategies and techniques agreed with the teacher. The advantage of this technique is that the pupils feel part of the learning process and can help to deliver a highly crafted and memorable experience. One disadvantage is that the extra level of planning requires additional time from both the teacher and pupils.

→ *The full teacher.* The pupil (or a group of pupils) is allocated a section of work and asked to deliver this to their classmates. The teacher will be available as a resource if needed, but their main role will be to present the material, evaluate its success and adapt support work as needed to ensure maximum learning from the class.

Resource 7E(ii) is intended for use in the staffroom, enabling the leadership group to request staff to identify any examples of the categories above and discuss their perceptions of how successful they are. Once you have collected this information, debate the topic within the leadership team, inviting some of the key exponents of the work to outline the pros and cons. Ideally involve pupils in this process too. Decide which of the techniques outlined (or any alternatives) you would like to see more of in your school.

It is important to involve the staff and pupils in reviewing the benefits (or not) of such work. Resource 7E(iii) contains a checklist of some of the advantages identified by Saga Briggs (2013). Use these prompts to analyse the peer-to-peer teaching in your school and share this information with all the staff. The wider the debate around the benefits, the more likely the staff and pupils in your school will feel brave enough to develop this aspect of their work.

Key questions

How often do pupils in your school take on the role of teacher?

Are you aware of the various types of peer-to-peer teaching in your school?

Do your staff discuss the benefits of peer-to-peer teaching?

How often do you ask pupils how they would improve their learning experience?

Resources (Download)

7E(i)	What do pupils remember about their last lesson?
7E(ii)	Finding examples of the 'pupil as teacher' in the school
7E(iii)	Identifying some of the benefits of peer-to-peer teaching

Developing evidence based practice

Why is this an important topic for conversation?

On what basis do professionals make the core judgements that inform their practice? This is a pivotal question for all practitioners – how do we know that we are working in a way that is the most appropriate, effective and in the best interests of our students? This is a moral debate about complex choices, but it is also a very pragmatic issue – what is the most cost-effective option, and which strategy is most likely to have the desired impact?

Key quotes for the section

> [J]ust a few decades ago, best medical practice was driven by things like eminence, charisma, and personal experience. We needed the help of statisticians, epidemiologists, information librarians, and experts in trial design to move forwards. Many doctors – especially the most senior ones – fought hard against this, regarding 'evidence based medicine' as a challenge to their authority.
>
> **(Goldacre, 2013: 4)**

> [M]any studies have little impact. They are small scale and serve to ensure an individual's or group's profile within a research community, which largely debates its own research activity, usually without any groundbreaking findings which could influence practice on a large scale.
>
> **(Waters, 2013: 229)**

8A

> The notion of teacher as researcher is important. [...] It is a refinement of the intelligent engagement in an 'educational practice'. It is a refreshing counterbalance to those who, in treating 'educational practice' as an object of science, necessarily fail to understand it. It is reassertion of the crucial place of professional judgement in an understanding of a professional activity.
>
> **(Pring, 2015: 163)**

Section discussion

It is very difficult to disagree with the view of research in education presented in the quote from Mick Waters. Even the most cursory overview of teacher activity reveals how limited is the time spent in any sort of engagement with research. However, this is not the case in every education system. In China, Japan and Singapore there is a very clear expectation that teachers will be active researchers as an integral part of their professional role.

One of the relatively less well understood aspects of educational practice in Finland is the emphasis on research based practice, which is exemplified in the pivotal concept of research based teacher education: 'Each student (teacher) [...] builds an understanding of the systemic, interdisciplinary nature of educational practice. Finnish students also acquire the skills of designing, conducting and presenting original research on practical or theoretical aspects of education' (Sahlberg, 2015: 116).

Three principles inform research based teacher education in Finland:

1 Teachers need a deep knowledge of the advances in research in the subjects they teach; they also need to be familiar with the research on teaching and learning.
2 Teachers' professional practice must be evidence based, using an analytical and open-minded approach and drawing on a range of sources of evidence as well as maintaining a critical perspective.
3 Teacher education should, of itself, be studied and investigated.

However, in many classrooms and leadership offices in other parts of the world there will be little, if any, evidence that there is even an awareness of research into professional practice. There are very strong cultural differences in both the norms informing professional practice and the creation of opportunities to engage in research. There is no real consensus in the UK about the nature and purpose of educational research, but it is probably best understood in terms of three distinct types of activity:

→ Research carried out by academics in universities and research organisations.

→ Research carried out by teachers for academic purposes (e.g. a higher degree).

→ Research carried out by teachers into their own practice as a professional development activity.

Use resource 8A(i) to analyse the current use of research in your school. If, as a leader, you are unable to complete this form accurately and independently, make gathering this information with your colleagues a priority for your work.

The basis for school based enquiry and research is very simple: what constitutes best practice? Just as with medical research, teaching practitioners need to be aware of research that might have implications for their own practice, shed light on the effectiveness of their own practice and contribute to the development of shared practice across the profession. In practical terms, an evidence based approach might include the following outcomes:

→ More accurate diagnosis of special needs and specific learning needs.

→ Review and analysis of teaching and learning strategies (e.g. Hattie, 2009).

→ Evaluation and review of school policy initiatives.

→ Cost–benefit analysis of the suitability of new resources.

→ Scientific research with implications for teaching and learning.

→ Challenging pseudoscience.

→ Improving practice through action research.

→ Testing and proving innovations.

Use resource 8A(ii) to consider where you already adopt any of these practices and how you could develop them further.

At a time of high stakes accountability, with sustained pressure to secure improvement *and* reduce resources, and the need for greater educational impact for the most disadvantaged and vulnerable young people, the case for better levels of sophistication in decision making seems unquestionable. However, there are real issues in terms of: the knowledge and skills required to conduct quality action research, the prevailing culture in many schools, the availability of resources and, not least, the time needed to develop a culture of enquiry and analysis.

The development of a culture of evidence based practice in a school would be facilitated by the adoption of some, if not all, of the following strategies:

→ Traditional course based CPD being replaced by dedicated time and resources to support action research (e.g. lesson study).

→ Senior staff supporting individual and group research through coaching.

→ The designation of a member of staff as a research coordinator to ensure access to research publications and to manage bids for funding.

→ Developing links with a local university to support research through access to staff and libraries, and to secure accreditation of school based activities.

→ Ensuring middle leaders are up to date with subject knowledge and pedagogic research.

→ Senior leaders working as a 'book club', agreeing to read and discuss a key text every term.

Resource 8A(iii) gives you the opportunity to introduce new strategies around evidence based practice. Add any additional ideas to the sheet and involve your staff in developing a plan of action to support this.

Any teacher would be appalled if their GP prescribed an inappropriate treatment on the basis that 'it might help'. The contraindications with any drug are at least as important as the potential benefits. Equally, a doctor's failure to be aware of the most recent findings in the treatment of a long-standing illness would be seen as professionally reprehensible. Education is not a science but there is abundant evidence as to what works and what does not. That distinction is central to medical practice – hence the injunction 'Do no harm'. Is the same true of education in your school?

Key questions

To what extent is professional practice in your school research based?

Who is responsible for the quality of research and evidence based practice in your school?

How far are you moving from CPD to JPD?

How systematic is the leadership team's use of evidence in informing key policy areas (e.g. spending the pupil premium)?

How available are key research texts for reference by teachers?

How open is your school to research based innovation?

Resources (Download)

8A(i)	Considering the approach to evidence based practice in your school
8A(ii)	Looking at best practice in your school
8A(iii)	Moving towards evidence based practice – an action plan

8B

B Research in the classroom

Why is this an important topic for conversation?

A large number of professional activities depend on evidence; indeed, it might be argued that for many professions work is the collection, analysis and identification of strategies using the appropriate evidence. Our very notion of justice is largely founded on the interpretation of evidence by judges and juries. The work of solicitors and barristers is fundamentally arguing over the relative veracity of witnesses and various types of evidence. Equally, medicine is a matter of diagnosis based on evidence followed by the identification of the most appropriate intervention strategies. Misdiagnosis or a failure to prescribe the best treatment can result in tragedy.

Professional practice in education is based on a wide range of sources – successful personal experience, modelling by senior staff, mentoring and rigorous analysis of what actually makes an impact on pupils' learning. This section discusses the case for a more robust approach to professional practice based on objective and reliable evidence.

Key quotes for the section

> There is a huge prize waiting to be claimed by teachers. By collecting better evidence about what works best, and establishing a culture where this evidence is used as a matter of routine, we can improve outcomes for children, and increase professional independence.
>
> **(Goldacre, 2013: 7)**

> The relationship between research and practice is not straightforward, in education as in any other professional field. There is no simple formula by which academic researchers produce research evidence for teachers to use in their classrooms. To begin with, in our country a systemic separation between the worlds of schools and universities has led people to claim that 'researchers are lost in thought; practitioners are missing in action'.
>
> **(Desforges, 2009: 4)**

Section discussion

Research in the classroom covers an enormous spectrum, from the individual teacher reflecting in a thoughtful and systematic way about her work with her class, to active participation in a major research project based on randomised controlled trials. Evidence based practice might be quantitative or qualitative, but it should always be underpinned by objectivity, authenticity, trustworthiness and relevance. It is important to develop an evidence based culture that respects multiple sources of evidence, in much the same way that a court of law takes DNA and alibis into account. Whatever the particular methodology adopted, it would seem to be self-evident that research in the classroom has an important part to play.

→ It can enhance a teacher's understanding of their own practice and provide data to support reflection, review and analysis. Most importantly, it can corroborate the teacher's intuitive sense of their own effectiveness.

→ It provides opportunities to test the validity and impact of resources and strategies and helps to build confidence in approaches that are actually making a difference (and abandon those not working as intended or claimed).

→ It allows teachers to take control of the improvement of their own practice, working with colleagues in a culture of high trust, interdependent collaboration and a commitment to long term development and improvement.

→ It places the emphasis on leaders to support development by making teaching and learning their key focus.

Perhaps the most appropriate, cost-effective and high impact strategy in terms of school based research is the approach broadly described as action research – that is, research into actual practice by teachers themselves. David Hargreaves argues for joint practice development as the answer to the problem of getting professional development to actually make a difference. He defines JPD as a process in which:

through mutual observation and coaching the donor reflects further on the practice that is being shared and explores ways in which it can be improved further. This is a process to which the recipient can also contribute as an act of reciprocity. In short, what begins as sharing practice ends up as a co-construction of practice that entails incremental innovation. [...] The term that most accurately describes this process is joint practice development, for it captures a process that

8B

is truly collaborative, not one-way; the practice is being improved, not just moved from one person or place to another. (Hargreaves, 2011: 10)

JPD can be seen as a direct alternative to traditional models of CPD. At its worst, CPD usually involves generic provision that is not directly related to actual classroom practice; it is run by experts and is very expensive. The power of Hargreaves' model is that it builds collaboration into the improvement process. This strengthens the case for collaboration in that it is not just structural but is also embedded in the day-to-day learning and relationships across the school.

The best known and most widely available model of JPD is lesson study:

Lesson Study is a breathtakingly simple and common sense way of developing teachers' practice knowledge: i.e. teachers' knowledge of how best to teach X to pupils like Y. In a Lesson Study, a group of teachers work together to plan, deliver and analyse a series of 'research lessons' devised to improve the way they teach something or the way particular learners learn something. (Dudley, 2013)

Lesson study is significant in a number of respects. Most importantly the process is owned by the teachers, who design and manage the research and implement the outcomes. Lesson study focuses professional development on improving actual practice by working in classrooms and solving practical problems. It is a strategy rooted in trust and focused on developing teachers as effective learners.

If one aspect of effective learning for pupils is to engage in collaborative problem solving (which is how they will spend most of their working lives), then there is a very strong case for involving pupils in research activities across the school as well as part of their curriculum experience. There is significant evidence to support the introduction of Philosophy for Children (P4C) into the curriculum. There is an interesting and significant link between the cognitive strategies and skills that P4C can help to develop and the skills required for research – for example, drawing a logically valid inference, analysing cause and effect, synthesising data and recognising the importance of trustworthiness in presenting evidence.

Pupils could be involved in the following research activities:

→ Evaluating their experience of a particular teaching and learning strategy.

→ Carrying out surveys on aspects of school life.

→ Participating in school improvement reviews.

→ Building significance and credibility into pupil voice activities.

→ Supporting peer review between schools.

Resource 8B(i) is a simple form to begin self-reflection on a particular lesson by a teacher. It should be used to encourage teachers to ask useful questions about their own practice, focusing on the effect of their own actions rather than just those of the pupils.

Resource 8B(ii) is for placing in the staffroom to collect evidence from the staff of examples of when they have used any of the strategies to involve pupils in research activities.

Gather the evidence and start thinking and talking the language of evidence informed practice. The changes will be clear!

Key questions

Is your school working towards evidence based practice?

To what extent is practitioner based research a norm in terms of your school's definition of effective classroom practice?

How far is your school's model of effective teaching and learning monitored by middle leaders in terms of consistency and improvement based on evidence?

Are pupils part of the research culture of your school?

Resources (Download)

8B(i) Supporting teacher analysis of their own practice in the classroom

8B(ii) Examples of pupils involved in research in the school (for use in the staffroom)

C   Using research to improve practice

Why is this an important topic for conversation?

Each day, a new article or research paper will appear from one erudite body or another. Each will shed new light on its own focus or problem. If you wait long enough, it is often possible to find two pieces of research which seem to arrive at completely different conclusions. How is this possible? Isn't research supposed to find the right answers?

Like most things in life, the answer lies not in extremes but in a balanced and considered approach to differing opinions. A teacher who reads a piece of educational research, sees a university logo, thinks 'This must be true' and then changes their practice to fit the new findings, is behaving just as irresponsibly as the teacher who adapts a position of disbelief on anything with 'research' in the title: 'What do that lot know about my pupils?'

This section will endeavour to assist you and your leadership team to adopt a healthy approach to considering new ideas, and also to help you see the weaknesses of some studies put out under the 'research' banner.

Key quotes for the section

> Research is about curiosity and inquiry, as for example journalism is. However, it differs from journalism in that it is governed by a number of expectations. There is the expectation that research will: aim to find new knowledge; be thorough; be balanced; be fair; be ethical.
>
> **(Thomas, 2013: 21)**

> Research can only tell us what has worked in a particular situation, not what will work in any future situation. The role of the educational professional in this process is not to translate general rules into particular lines of action. It is rather to use research findings to make one's problem solving more intelligent.
>
> **(Biesta, 2007)**

> [R]esearch can help us to gain new insights, but it rarely leads to solid, universal conclusions.
>
> **(Wood and Smith, 2016: 3)**

> A specialist is a man who knows more and more about less and less.
>
> **(attributed to William J. Mayo)**

> Shall we educate ourselves in what is known, and then casting away all we have acquired, turn to our ignorance for aid to guide us among the unknown?
>
> **(Faraday, 2005 [1859]: 328)**

Section discussion

Developing a healthy respect for the plethora of educational research which is now available at the push of a button is perhaps one of the most valuable things that you (and the rest of your team) can do. With the advent of academic search engines (e.g. https://scholar.google.co.uk), it is now possible to access the combined brain power of thousands of very intelligent people. Who in their right mind would want to ignore this huge resource? Equally, who would be daft enough to dip their metaphorical toe into this crowded pool, choose the first bit of research they meet and accept everything it contains as hard fact? The high quality school will adopt a position somewhere between these two points.

The first part of developing the school's relationship with research is to know where to find it. There are a number of search engines which enable you to quickly access thousands of articles, many of which require a further subscription to download them. Some universities are very keen to help schools develop their expertise in this area, and a quick call to your local department of education may well lead to some helpful tips, although anyone completing an MA/MSc will most likely already have enhanced access to their university's own libraries (both virtual and physical). Various educational magazines and blogs also highlight new pieces of research.

Resource 8C(i) offers a grid for use by the leadership team to consider what aspects of the school's work would actually benefit from a research slant. Leadership team discussion on this will enable you to prioritise the needs of the school and its pupils.

When you begin to collect your research, the papers that initially surface may not be the best, the most accurate or the most appropriate for your needs. It is important to develop an approach which will enable you to decide if a piece of research is worthy of further consideration. The following questions may help you prioritise the work you want to focus on.

What question are they trying to answer?

Just because a piece of research pops up from a key word search, it does not necessarily mean that it is relevant to the area you are exploring. Read the abstract carefully: are they actually trying to shed light on the area you are interested in? Ask yourself: even if this research is the most accurate and most expertly undertaken in the world, would the findings benefit our school? If not, then look further.

When did they do this?

Search engines do not return research papers in chronological order unless you set this as a search criteria; instead they will match to key words. This means the first paper you read could be over 30 years old. Clearly, this does not mean it is invalid, but if it is useful you may well find it cited (and enhanced) in more recent research. (It is quite interesting to look at trends in research. When you do, you will often see the same issues coming up in 20 to 30 year cycles.)

What is the reason for the research?

Some research is for the general widening of knowledge. Sometimes doctoral students will alight on a topic because it offers them the potential to demonstrate their research prowess. Some research is undertaken because the researcher is driven to find the solution to an issue that is causing them concern. A further category is sponsored or funded research: this is where individuals are paid to carry out research for a particular group or company. This link should be declared in the acknowledgements section.

It would be wrong to rule out any of these types of research as invalid, but it would be equally wrong not to consider the potential for bias. The food industry, for example, is full of contradictory research from competing lobbies, with some very concerning reports emerging on the efficacy of some claims made in the sugar vs. fat debate. Closer to home, any research showing that pupils using 'Product A' made quicker progress than those not using it should be approached with scepticism. Don't make the mistake made by some politicians who visit successful schools/education systems and report on 'what' has caused its success (usually one of their pet themes), often ignoring the bigger 'how' that was actually at the root of their progress!

What is the size of the research?

It is not a straight line correlation that bigger research is better, but it is easy to see that research based on a small sample taken over a short period of time should be scrutinised very closely. For this reason, people are often drawn to meta-research where the findings are drawn from analysing a broad range of studies.

What are the demographics of the subjects of the research?

Anyone involved with education will know that any two groups of students, even within the same school, can be very different. Once the comparison occurs across different areas of the world or across different social and cultural conditions, the transferability of findings becomes a significant issue. While the only way to find research totally applicable to your own class is to carry out action research (see topic 8B), with care it is possible to find studies which may have interesting implications for your own work.

Are they looking for the right thing?

The current worldwide race to improve assessment test performance has resulted in some research which is very focused on finding the best way to do this. This raises some difficult questions for educationalists. For example, if a piece of research were to show that standing upside down on their heads increased pupils' test performance, should this be considered by a school, even though the research did not consider the long term effect on pupil health or mental well-being? Sometimes just knowing the answer to the question is not enough.

Using this set of questions is a good way to begin interrogating the research you are considering. The questions are placed into a grid for your use in resource 8C(ii). Use this to check on the appropriateness of any identified research for your school and its situation.

Once you have found a piece of research that you think is going to support your journey ahead, share it widely among the staff – not as the answer to all your prayers but as something to help you in your journey. Rarely does research hold all the answers, but it may assist you to ask the important questions.

8C

Key questions

Do you know where to find the latest research?

Do you regularly check the validity of the research you are looking at?

Do you check the transferability of the research you are considering?

Once you have identified research that is useful for your school, what do you do?

Do you encourage all your staff to take a healthy interest in the research available?

Resources (Download)

8C(i) What questions do you want research help on?
8C(ii) Analysing the research

D   Taking evidence from outside the education world

Why is this an important topic for conversation?

Individuals in some sectors of education will instinctively sneer when anyone brings a piece of research, or even an idea, from outside the sealed world of education. There is a reflex response which suggests that no one without direct experience of teaching in a school has the authority to comment on it. This is a very limiting view of the world.

New materials are published almost every day; whether it is business guidance for leading others, advice on ways to get your message across or self-help books on how to gain more self-confidence, lots of publications can contain valuable ideas or thinking. The potential size of these markets far exceeds those of education, hence they provide more incentive to authors/researchers to dedicate their thinking to work in these areas. Of course, this does not mean that all of this material is either valuable or accurate; however, the converse is equally incorrect. Reading the latest bestselling 'improve your business' book might not seem the natural choice when you consider your cramped schedule, but it just might get you thinking about your own work in a different way.

Key quotes for the section

> In the search to understand so much failure, a lot of blame gets assigned. One health care executive commented, 'We're under so much stress that all we do is look around the organization to find somebody we can shoot.' [...] It's become commonplace to say that people resist change, that the organization lacks the right people to move it into the future, that people no longer assume responsibility for their work, that people are too dependent, that all they do is whine.
>
> Can we put a stop to all this slander and the ill will it's creating in our organizations? Most organizational change failures are the result of some deep misunderstandings of who people are and what's going on inside organizations. If we can clear up these misunderstandings, effectiveness and hope can return to our work. Successful organizational change is possible if we look at our organizational experience with new eyes.
>
> **(Wheatley, 2007: 83)**

> More often than not, when misunderstandings or conflicts occur amongst people, it's usually someone else's fault. If only *they* had listened. If only *they* communicated things more clearly. If only *they* understood me better.
>
> One of the biggest breakdowns at work is not a lack of technical skill or knowledge. It's not bad processes or too much red tape. The biggest problem is breakdowns in relationship whether it's with our colleagues, bosses or clients.
>
> **(Burns, 2015: 135; original emphasis)**

> So conscience is essentially intuitive. To anticipate what is not yet, but is to be made real, conscience must be based on intuition. And it is in this sense that conscience may be called irrational. But is not conscience in this respect analogous to love? Is not love just as irrational, just as intuitive? In fact, love does intuit, for it also envisions something that is not yet real. What love anticipates, however, is not an ethical necessity but, rather, a personal possibility. Love reveals potentialities dormant in the loved person that he still has to make real.
>
> **(Frankl, 2000: 40)**

Section discussion

Work and stress levels in schools have never been higher. Teachers and leaders are facing fresh demands on them every year. In some instances, this increase in tempo has caused a narrowing of the scope of schooling. When a leader simply does not have enough time to complete all the tasks in a day, they will often turn to traditional ways to solve new problems. For many schools, particularly those on the edge of crisis, they instinctively look to see how other schools have achieved success. In effect, they will search within the education bubble for a solution, assuming this is where the quickest results are to be found. This may be true, but it may well be ignoring other very rich sources of ideas and thinking.

For many teaching staff, education is the only reality they have ever known. They were a pupil, then a student, then a teacher – education is their world. The benefit of looking outside that sphere for answers is that a fresh perspective sometimes allows schools to approach a problem in a completely different way.

For example, if a school is in difficulty and the systems introduced to solve their problems simply aren't working, the quote from Chantal Burns might just induce a leader to see the issue in another way. Perhaps, in the drive to change things, the team has unintentionally damaged relationships within the organisation. Perhaps, rather than obsessing about the 'what', they should devote more time to the 'why'. Another school may find the extensive writings of Margaret Wheatley on the effect of change on society a very useful tool to help staff understand why they feel unsettled or insecure.

Some schools have used *Eat That Frog!* by Brian Tracy (2013) as a way to encourage their staff to be brave. The book is mainly targeted at individual effectiveness and, like many successful pieces of work, the central message is a simple one. Tracy says that people tend to put off doing the difficult/unpleasant things, so if you had to eat a live frog every day (a universally repulsive act), if the frog was eaten first thing in the morning then the rest of the day would be much more positive and productive. Some school leadership teams have taken this approach to heart and have integrated this language into their daily lives: 'Have you eaten your frog yet?' 'This is my frog for tomorrow' and so on. This type of thinking has enabled schools to address educational issues in non-traditional ways.

Use this section to increase the awareness of the potential benefits to be gained by looking outside the sphere of education for solutions. Try not to tackle this as another piece of bureaucracy but rather as an enjoyable team activity. One way to introduce this would be to dedicate a team meeting to the topic. Ask each member of the team to find a piece of work from outside the education world that interests them. For those who feel unable to identify anything themselves, a simple solution is to take a trip to the nearest bookshop, raid the business/self-help book shelves and then distribute them around the team via a 'lucky dip'. Using resource 8D(i), ask everyone to review their book (or article, webpage, video, etc.) and consider its possible use within your own school setting. When the information is presented at the leadership meeting, ensure copies of the completed forms are available and that a strict time restriction is placed on receiving the feedback.

Use resource 8D(ii) to summarise the discussions of the group and attempt to place the readings in order of the potential benefit they could offer your school. Try to avoid scepticism becoming a habitual behaviour of the group. Look at the potential of the work, and bear in mind that the only benefit you might derive from it may be a phrase or attitude which can be developed in the context of your school. It is possible to extract wisdom from almost anything, even if that wisdom is how *not* to do something!

8D

Key questions

Do you ever look for answers outside education?

Do you regularly talk about new ideas within your leadership team?

Are you prepared to think outside your normal constraints?

What are the biggest issues you need to solve?

What new writing might help you on your journey?

Resources (Download)

8D(i)   Looking at non-educational resources
8D(ii)   Gathering and prioritising the readings of the leadership team

E   Some research of note

Why is this an important topic for conversation?

Any activity as complex, significant and expensive as education will attract a wide range of claims as to how to ensure best outcomes and optimal levels of success. However, education is not a science. It sits, often uncomfortably, between cognitive science, psychology and elements of the social sciences. There is always a very high personal element to statements about the nature and purpose of education, and the debate is as much political and moral as it is personal.

There is no single authoritative view as to a definitive model of teaching and learning. Into such ambiguity emerges a wide range of remedies and solutions.

Key quote for the section

> Many myths in education arise from overly simple categorisation and stereotyping. We probably all have a notion of what we mean by 'traditional' or 'progressive' education, but to make any meaningful comparison of the effectiveness of each requires more than a woolly notion. The characteristics of each need to be described, and the influence of each characteristic on educational outcomes needs to be separately addressed.
>
> **(Adey and Dillon, 2012: xxiii)**

Section discussion

The growth of the evidence base in education, particularly for teaching and learning, has led to a wide ranging debate that covers the spectrum of trustworthiness. On the one hand there is hard edged empirical science, and on the other what might be charitably described as well-intentioned speculative thinking. The range covers everything from cognitive neuroscience to Brain Gym. Just as medical practice is plagued by unscientific theories, so education has its fair share of nostrums – not to mention snake oil. Just as medicine seeks a universal panacea, so too does education.

Although there are real issues in the application of what might be described as mainstream science to educational practice, there are some useful examples of how our understanding of science might inform teaching and learning. For example, from the perspective of cognitive neuroscience, Sarah-Jayne Blakemore and Uta Frith state:

It is unlikely that there is one single all-purpose type of learning for everything. In terms of brain structures involved, learning mathematics differs from learning to read, which differs from learning to play the piano. (Blakemore and Frith, 2005: 139)

Robert Plomin, on the other hand, is a geneticist. He observes:

[C]hildren who find mastery of skills difficult are, in almost all cases, not genetically distinct from other children. There is no genetic reason why they cannot succeed given personalized support. These pupils need to be taught in a way that makes sense to them, and their precise level of understanding at the beginning of the learning process has to be identified in order for education and skill formation to progress in a logical, hierarchical sequence. Supporting these children should be the top priority for all schools. (Asbury and Plomin, 2014: 162)

The work of the Sutton Trust and the EEF is probably the most influential source of evidence based practice in England at present. Their analysis of effective teaching and learning, in terms of pupil progress and cost–benefit, provides a major resource for decision making in schools, particularly with regard to the allocation of pupil premium resources. However, their work has been controversial – largely because it seems counterintuitive to many teachers. For example, in the *Toolkit of Strategies to Improve Learning* (2011), Higgins and colleagues summarise various strategies:

→ On effective feedback: 'One study even estimates that the impact of rapid feedback on learning is 124 times more cost effective that reducing class sizes' (p. 14).

→ On metacognitive approaches: Studies report 'substantial gains equivalent to moving a class from 50th place in a league table of 100 schools to about 25th' (p. 22).

→ On teaching assistants: 'Most studies have consistently found very small or no effects on attainment' (p. 31).

→ On school uniforms: 'There is no robust evidence that introducing a school uniform will improve academic performance' (p. 28).

→ On reducing class sizes: 'Overall the benefits are not particularly large or clear, until class size is reduced to under 20 or even below 15' (p. 27).

Resource 8E(i) offers the above list in a format that invites your leadership team to think about their opinions on each of these topics. Remember that the process of leadership must include opportunities for debate and disagreement. It is worth remembering that even the most rigorous research is subject to personal values and emotional responses.

For example, intelligent, thoughtful and scientifically literate people who smoke are often in absolute denial that the research on the effects of smoking actually applies to them.

Another highly authoritative study was led by John Hattie (2009). Synthesising the results of over 800 studies, Hattie identified the teacher attributes that have a marked and meaningful effect on student learning, and those that don't. As a result of his analysis, Hattie argues two things: (1) the evidence that makes a difference to teaching and learning must be located at the 'teacher' level, and (2) we should implement the strategies that are shown to enhance achievement by more than the average for educational research (a 0.40 effect size). Hattie's model of Visible Learning is highly influential and meets the most rigorous criteria for validity and reliability.

In direct contrast to the Sutton Trust and John Hattie, there are the range of theories and strategies that do not meet the criteria for academic or professional acceptability or integrity. Perhaps the most extreme example of a theory with no evidence to corroborate its applicability is the portfolio of strategies known as Brain Gym. While it is probably a good idea to have the occasional break from studying to move around and have a laugh, there is no evidence to justify the claims made for Brain Gym.

The same is true of learning styles. Frank Coffield (2012: 228) observes: 'The study of learning styles has led me to conclude that all of us need a strong dose of healthy scepticism to help us lose our reverence for some of the material that is presented to us on staff development days. In our research learning style instruments have been shown to be unreliable, invalid and of negligible impact on practice.'

Brain Gym and learning styles will do no harm to your pupils, although they will usually not do what they claim to do. For children faced with many hours in the same building, doing essentially the same thing, it is clear that some degree of variety is beneficial. When we are on a long drive on a motorway, we rarely remember the details of the journey. So, looking for the new and the different must be applauded, but not without taking a great deal of care.

Tom Bennett provides powerful advice on the whole business of research in education:

Try to achieve something as close to a scientific model as possible, and when this is not possible, don't just write it off as irrelevant, or ignore it. Report your sample size. How did you obtain the data? Whom did you ask? How did you ensure that bias was minimised? When you come to write your conclusions, are your summaries more wish fulfilment than what the data is actually saying? (Bennett, 2013: 200)

Resource 8E(ii) is available to use as a way of recording your findings in a more scientific way. Bring these forms regularly to the leadership team. Share your thoughts, ideas and learning, working together to try to ensure that individual bias is minimised.

Key questions

How confident are you in the validity, reliability and trustworthiness of the research that is used in your school?

Has the issue of unreliable research ever been discussed as part of professional development?

Has your school spent any money on panaceas or nostrums? How can you avoid making the same mistake in the future?

Resources (Download)

8E(i) Thinking about some challenging findings – some provocations to promote discussion among the leadership team

8E(ii) Focusing on scientific method

References and further reading

Adey, P. and Dillon, J. (eds) (2012). *Bad Education: Debunking Myths in Education*. Maidenhead: Open University Press.

Alexander, R. J. and Armstrong, M. (2010). *Children, Their World, Their Education: Final Report and Recommendations of the Cambridge Primary Review*. Abingdon: Routledge.

Allen, M. B. (2005). *Eight Questions on Teacher Recruitment and Retention: What Does the Research Say?* Denver, CO: Education Commission of the States. Available at: http://files.eric.ed.gov/fulltext/ED489332.pdf.

Anderson, M. (2013). Teacher Confidence in Using Technology, *ICT Evangelist* (8 September). Available at: https://ictevangelist.com/teacher-confidence-using-technology/.

Asbury, K. and Plomin, R. (2014). *G is for Genes*. Chichester: Wiley.

Beland, L-P. and Murphy, R. (2015). Ill Communication: Technology, Distraction & Student Performance. CEP Discussion Paper No. 1350. Available at: http://cep.lse.ac.uk/pubs/download/dp1350.pdf.

Bennett, T. (2013). *Teacher Proof*. Abingdon: Routledge.

Biesta, G. (2007). Why 'What Works' Won't Work: Evidence-Based Practice and the Democratic Deficit in Educational Research, *Educational Theory* 57(1): 1–22. Available at: http://onlinelibrary.wiley.com/doi/10.1111/j.1741-5446.2006.00241.x/full.

Blakemore, S-J. and Frith, U. (2005). *The Learning Brain: Lessons for Education*. Oxford: Blackwell.

Bowers, C. A. (2011). *Let Them Eat Data: How Computers Affect Education, Cultural Diversity, and the Prospects of Ecological Sustainability*. Athens, GA: University of Georgia Press.

Briggs, S. (2013). How Peer Teaching Improves Student Learning and 10 Ways To Encourage It, *InformED* (7 June). Available at: http://www.opencolleges.edu.au/informed/features/peer-teaching/.

Brighouse, T. and Woods, D. (1999). *How to Improve Your School*. Abingdon: Routledge.

Brinkman, S. A., Johnson, S. E., Codde, J., Hart, M. B., Straton, J., Mittinty, M. N. and Silburn, S. R. (2016). Efficacy of Infant Simulator Programmes to Prevent Teenage Pregnancy: A School-Based Cluster Randomised Controlled Trial in Western Australia, *The Lancet* 388(10057): 2264–2271. Available at: http://doi.org/10.1016/S0140-6736(16)30384-1.

Britland, M. (2016). A Blend of Tech and Tradition is Best for Schools, *Your Ready Business* (22 April). Available at: https://www.yourreadybusiness.co.uk/blend-tech-tradition-best-schools/?utm_content=buffer82478%20andutm_medium=social%20andutm_source=twitter.com%20andutm_campaign=buffer.

Burns, C. (2015). *Instant Motivation: The Surprising Truth Behind What Really Drives Top Performers*. Harlow: Pearson Education.

Caine, R. N., Caine, G., McClintic, C. and Klimek, K. J. (2009). *12 Brain/Mind Learning Principles in Action: Developing Executive Functions of the Human Brain*. Thousand Oaks, CA: Corwin/SAGE.

Callaghan, J. (1976). A Rational Debate Based on the Facts. Speech given at Ruskin College, Oxford, 18 October. Available at: http://www.educationengland.org.uk/documents/speeches/1976ruskin.html.

Carney, K. (2008). Making Meetings Work, *Sirius Meetings*. Available at: http://www.siriusmeetings.com/articles/article-making-meetings-work.

Chomsky, N. (2000). *Chomsky on Miseducation*. Lanham, MD: Rowman and Littlefield.

Cladingbowl, M. (2013). The Key Role of Middle Leaders: An Ofsted Perspective, *Teaching Leaders Quarterly* (November): 5–7.

Clark, C. and Dugdale, G. (2008). Literacy Changes Lives: The Role of Literacy in Offending Behaviour – A Discussion Piece. Part 1. National Literacy Trust. Available at: https://lemosandcrane.co.uk/resources/NLT%20-%20The%20role%20of%20literacy%20in%20offending%20behaviour.pdf.

Coats, S. (n.d.). Time Management for Developing Leaders, *The Leadership Challenge*. Available at: http://www.leadershipchallenge.com/resource/time-management-for-developing-leaders.aspx.

Coe, R., Aloisi, C., Higgins, S. and Elliot Major, L. (2014). *What Makes Great Teaching? Review of the Underpinning Research*. London: Sutton Trust. Available at: http://www.suttontrust.com/wp-content/uploads/2014/10/What-makes-great-teaching-FINAL-4.11.14.pdf.

Coffield, F. (2012). Learning Styles: Unreliable, Invalid, Impractical and Yet Still Widely Used, in P. Adey and J. Dillon (eds), *Bad Education: Debunking Myths in Education*. Maidenhead: Open University Press, pp. 215–230.

Covey, S. R. (2004). *The 7 Habits of Highly Effective People*. New York: Free Press.

Covey, S. R. (2006). *The Speed of Trust*. New York: Simon & Schuster.

Cunningham, R. and Lewis, K. (2012). *NFER Teacher Voice Omnibus 2012 Survey: The Use of the Pupil Premium*. Slough: NFER.

Darling-Hammond, L. and Lieberman, A. (eds) (2012). *Teacher Education Around the World: Changing Policies and Practices*. Abingdon: Routledge.

Department for Education (DfE) (2014). *Promoting Fundamental British Values As Part of SMSC in Schools: Departmental Advice for Maintained Schools*. London: DfE. Available at: https://www.gov.uk/government/publications/promoting-fundamental-british-values-through-smsc.

Department for Education (DfE) (2015). *Permanent and Fixed-Period Exclusions in England: 2013 to 2014*. Ref: SFR 28/2015. Available at: https://www.gov.uk/government/statistics/permanent-and-fixed-period-exclusions-in-england-2013-to-2014.

Desforges, C. (2009). Foreword, in A. Morris, *Evidence Matters: Towards Informed Professionalism for Educators*. Reading: CfBT Education Trust, pp. 3–4. Available at: https://www.educationdevelopmenttrust.com/~/media/EDT/Reports/Research/2009/r-evidence-matters-2009.pdf.

Dewey, J. (1938). *Experience and Education*. New York: Macmillan.

Doyle, M. and Straus, D. (1993). *How to Make Meetings Work: The New Interaction Method*. New York: Jove Books.

Dudley, P. (2013). The Power of Teachers Carrying Out Lesson Study, *SecEd* (28 February). Available at: http://www.sec-ed.co.uk/blog/the-power-of-teachers-carrying-out-lesson-study.

Dunbar, A. (2010). *How Many Friends Does One Person Need? Dunbar's Number and Other Evolutionary Quirks*. London: Faber & Faber.

Duncan, G. J. and Murnane, R. J. (eds) (2011). *Whither Opportunity: Rising Inequality, Schools, and Children's Life Chances*. New York: Russell Sage Foundation.

Dweck, C. (2006). *Mindset: The New Psychology of Success*. New York: Ballantine Books.

EF Explore America (2012). What is 21st Century Education? [video]. Available at: https://www.youtube.com/watch?v=Ax5cNlutAys.

Elmore, R. F. (2000). *Building a New Structure for School Leadership*. Washington, DC: Albert Shanker Institute. Available at: http://files.eric.ed.gov/fulltext/ED546618.pdf.

Erstad, O. (2010). Educating the Digital Generation, *Nordic Journal of Digital Literacy* 10: 85–102. Available at: https://www.idunn.no/dk/2015/Jubileumsnummer/educating_the_digital_generation_-_exploring_media_literacy.

Evans, G. (2006). *Educational Failure and Working Class White Children in Britain*. Basingstoke: Palgrave.

Everard, B. and Morris, G. (1996). *Effective School Management* (3rd edn). London: Paul Chapman.

Faraday, M. (2005 [1859]). *Experimental Researches in Chemistry and Physics*. London: Taylor and Francis.

Flinders, D. J., Uhrmacher, P. B. and Moroye, C. M. (2013). *Curriculum and Teaching Dialogue*. Vol. 15, 1 & 2. Greenwich, CT: Information Age Publishing.

Flintham, A. (2010). *Reservoirs of Hope: Sustaining Spirituality in School Leaders*. Newcastle upon Tyne: Cambridge Scholars Publishing.

Frankl, V. E. (2000). *Man's Search for Ultimate Meaning*. New York: Basic Books.

Fullan, M. (2006). *Turnaround Leadership*. San Francisco, CA: Jossey-Bass.

Fullan, M. (2013). *Stratosphere: Integrating Technology, Pedagogy, and Change Knowledge*. Toronto: Pearson.

Gates, B. (2014). Software Breakthroughs: Solving the Toughest Problems in Computer Science. Speech given at the University of Illinois, Urbana–Champaign, 24 February.

Gilbert, I. (2013). *Independent Thinking*. Carmarthen: Independent Thinking Press.

GMSA (2017). Number of Global Mobile Subscribers to Surpass Five Billion this Year, Finds New GSMA Study [press release] (27 February). Available at: https://www.gsma.com/newsroom/press-release/number-of-global-mobile-subscribers-to-surpass-five-billion-this-year/.

Goldacre, B. (2013). Building Evidence Into Education. Available at: http://media.education.gov.uk/assets/files/pdf/b/ben%20goldacre%20paper.pdf.

Gopnic, A. (2016). *The Gardener and the Carpenter: What the New Science of Child Development Tells Us About the Relationship Between Parents and Children*. London: Bodley Head.

Guarino, C. M., Santibañez, L. and Daley, G. A. (2006). Teacher Recruitment and Retention: A Review of the Recent Empirical Literature, *Review of Educational Research* 76(2): 173–208. DOI: https://doi.org/10.3102/00346543076002173.

Gutman, L. M. and Vorhaus, J. (2012). The Impact of Pupil Behaviour and Wellbeing on Educational Outcomes. Research Brief: DFE-RB253. London: Department for Education. Available at: https://www.gov.uk/government/publications/the-impact-of-pupil-behaviour-and-wellbeing-on-educational-outcomes.

Hardison, J. (2013). Part 1: 44 Smart Ways to Use Smartphones in Class, *Getting Smart* (7 January). Available at: http://www.gettingsmart.com/2013/01/part-1-44-smart-ways-to-use-smartphones-in-class/.

Hargreaves, A., Boyle, A. and Harris, A. (2014). *Uplifting Leadership*. San Francisco, CA: Jossey-Bass.

Hargreaves, A., Halász, G. and Pont, B. (2008). The Finnish Approach to System Leadership, in B. Pont, D. Nusche and D. Hopkins (eds), *Improving School Leadership*. Vol. 2: *Case Studies on System Leadership*. Paris: OECD, pp. 69–109.

Hargreaves, A. and Shirley, D. (2009). *The Fourth Way: The Inspiring Future for Educational Change*. Thousand Oaks, CA: Corwin.

Hargreaves, D. H. (2010). *Creating a Self-Improving School System*. Nottingham: National College for Leadership of Schools and Children's Services. Available at: http://dera.ioe.ac.uk/2093/1/download%3Fid%3D133672%26filename%3Dcreating-a-self-improving-school-system.pdf.

Hargreaves, D. H. (2011). *Leading a Self-Improving School System*. Nottingham: National College for Teaching and Leadership.

Harris, B. (2007). *Supporting the Emotional Work of School leaders*. London: Paul Chapman.

Harris, S. D. (2009). Q&A: Marc Benioff, CEO of Salesforce.com, *Mercury News* (23 October). Available at: http://www.mercurynews.com/2009/10/23/2009-qa-marc-benioff-ceo-of-salesforce-com/.

Haslam, A., Reicher. S. and Platow, M. (2011). *The New Psychology of Leadership: Identity, Influence, and Power*. New York: Psychology Press.

Hattie, J. (2009). *Visible Learning: A Synthesis of Over 800 Meta-Analyses Relating to Achievement*. Abingdon and New York: Routledge.

Higgins, S., Kokotsaki, D. and Coe, R. (2011). *Toolkit of Strategies to Improve Learning: Summary for Schools Spending the Pupil Premium*. London: Sutton Trust. Available at: http://www.cem.org/attachments/1toolkit-summary-final-r-2-.pdf.

Inman, H. (2013). Time Management 101: Stop Managing Time, *Forbes* (20 December). Available at: https://www.forbes.com/sites/hennainam/2013/12/20/time-management-101-stop-managing-time/#6ae1dd0f24f9.

Irish National Teachers' Organization (INTO) (1996). *Effective School Leadership*. Dublin: INTO. Available at: https://www.into.ie/ROI/Publications/PublicationsPre2000/EffectiveSchoolOrganisation1996.pdf.

Jindal-Snape, D. and Miller, D. J. (2008). A Challenge of Living? Understanding the Psycho-Social Processes of the Child During Primary–Secondary Transition Through Resilience and Self-Esteem Theories, *Educational Psychology Review* 20(3): 217–236.

Jukes, I., McCain, T. and Crockett, L. (2010). *Understanding the Digital Generation: Teaching and Learning in the New Digital Landscape*. Vancouver, BC: 21st Century Fluency Project.

Kelly, F. S., McCain, T. and Crockett, L. (2009). *Teaching the Digital Generation*. Thousand Oaks, CA: Corwin.

Kiema, K. (2015). As Schools Lift Bans on Cell Phones, Educators Weigh Pros and Cons, *NEA Today* (23 February). Available at: http://neatoday.org/2015/02/23/school-cell-phone-bans-end-educators-weigh-pros-cons/.

Lambert, L. (1998). Building Leadership Capacity in Schools. APC Monograph No. 1. Hawthorn, VIC: Australian Principals Centre.

Leithwood, K. and Riehl, C. (2003). What We Know About Successful School Leadership. Philadelphia, PA: Laboratory for Student Success, Temple University. Available at: http://olms.cte.jhu.edu/olms2/data/ck/file/What_we_know_about_SchoolLeadership.pdf.

Leithwood, K., Day, C., Sammons, P., Harris, A. and Hopkins D. (2006). *Seven Strong Claims About Successful School Leadership*. Nottingham: National College for Teaching and Leadership.

Lencioni, P. M. (2002). *The Five Dysfunctions of a Team: A Leadership Fable*. San Francisco, CA: Jossey-Bass.

Levin, B. (2008). *How to Change 5000 Schools: A Practical and Positive Approach*. Cambridge, MA: Harvard Education Press.

Lowe, J. (2007). *Jack Welch Speaks: Wit and Wisdom from the World's Greatest Business Leader*. Hoboken, NJ: John Wiley.

Lupton, R. (2004). Schools in Disadvantaged Areas: Recognising Context and Raising Quality. LSE STICERD Research Paper No. CASE076. Available at: https://ssrn.com/abstract=1158967.

MacAskill, W. (2015). *Doing Good Better: Effective Altruism and a Radical New Way to Make a Difference*. London: Guardian Books.

Macleod, S., Sharp, C., Bernardinelli, D., Skipp, A. and Higgins, S. (2015). Supporting the Attainment of Disadvantaged Pupils: Articulating Success and Good Practice. Research Report (November). London: Department for Education. Available at: https://www.nfer.ac.uk/publications/pupp01.

Mandinach, E. B. and Cline, H. F. (1993). *Classroom Dynamics: Implementing a Technology-based Learning Environment*. Hillsdale, NJ: Lawrence Erlbaum Associates.

Maslow, A. H. (1943). A Theory of Human Motivation, *Psychological Review* 50: 370–396.

Meader, M. (2016). The Value of Promoting Respect in Schools, *Thought Co.* (24 September). Available at: http://teaching.about.com/od/SchoolPolicy/a/Respect-In-Schools.htm.

Mitra, S. (2014). *The Educators*, BBC Radio 4 (17 September). Available at: http://www.bbc.co.uk/programmes/b04gvm7n.

Mulholland, D. J., Watt, N. F., Philpott, A. and Sarlin, N. (1991). Academic Performance in Children of Divorce: Psychological Resilience and Vulnerability, *Psychiatry* 54(3): 268–280.

NAHT (2013). Leaders and Learners – Shaping the Future [conference programme]. Available at: http://www.naht.org.uk/EasysiteWeb/getresource.axd?AssetID=34684.

Nelson, T. and Quinn, S. (2016). Ensuring Middle Leaders Make a Positive Difference. Presentation at the Inspiring Leadership Conference, International Convention Centre, Birmingham, 15–17 June. Available at: http://www.inspiringleadership.org/images/uploads/Ensuring_Middle_Leaders_Make_a_Positive_Difference_-_Tim_Nelson_Sarah_Quinn.pdf.

Noguera, P. (2008). *The Trouble with Black Boys … And Other Reflections on Race, Equity, and the Future of Public Education*. San Francisco, CA: Jossey-Bass.

O'Brien, J. (2016). *Don't Send Him in Tomorrow*. Carmarthen: Independent Thinking Press.

O'Rourke, J. S. and Yarbrough, B. T. (2008). *Module 1: Leading Groups and Teams* (2nd edn). Mason, OH: South-Western Cengage Learning.

Ofsted (2016). *School Inspection Handbook* (August). Ref: 150066. Available at: https://www.gov.uk/government/uploads/system/uploads/attachment_data/file/553942/School_inspection_handbook-section_5.pdf.

Organisation for Economic Co-operation and Development (OECD) (2015). *Education Policy Outlook 2015: Making Reforms Happen*. Paris: OECD.

Ormiston, M. (2013). How to Use Cell Phones as Learning Tools, *Teach Hub*. Available at: http://www.teachhub.com/how-use-cell-phones-learning-tools.

Orpinas, P. and Horne, A. M. (2009). Creating a Positive School Climate and Developing Social Competence, in S. R. Jimerson, S. M. Swearer and D. L. Espelage (eds), *Handbook of Bullying in Schools: An International Perspective*. New York: Routledge, pp. 49–60.

PBS (2001). Commanding Heights [interview with Mikhail Gorbachev]. Available at: https://www.pbs.org/wgbh/commandingheights/shared/minitext/int_mikhailgorbachev.html.

Penn, W. (1903 [1682]). *Some Fruits of Solitude*. Westminster: Archibald, Constable & Co. Available at: https://archive.org/details/somefruitsofsoli00penniala.

Perkins, D. N. (2014). *Future Wise: Educating Our Children for a Changing World*. San Francisco, CA: Jossey-Bass.

Pinker, S. (2015). *The Village Effect: Why Face-to-Face Contact Matters*. London: Atlantic Books.

Prensky, M. (2001). Digital Natives, Digital Immigrants, *On the Horizon* 9(5): 1–6.

Pridham, S. (2014). *Freaked Out: The Bewildered Teacher's Guide to Digital Learning*. Carmarthen: Independent Thinking Press.

Pring, R. (2013). *The Life and Death of Secondary Education for All*. Abingdon: Routledge.

Pring, R. (2015). *The Philosophy of Educational Research* (3rd edn). London: Bloomsbury.

Putnam, R. (2015). *Our Kids: The American Dream in Crisis*. New York: Simon & Schuster.

Ramey, K. (2012). The Pros and Cons of Cell Phones in Schools, *Use of Technology* (10 December). Available at: https://www.useoftechnology.com/pros-cons-cell-phones-schools/.

Reimers, F. and McGinn, N. F. (1997). *Informed Dialogue: Using Research to Shape Education Policy Around the World*. Westport, CT: Praeger.

Roberson, J. (2012). *The Discipline Coach*. Carmarthen: Independent Thinking Press.

Robinson, K. and Aronica, L. (2010). *The Element: How Finding Your Passion Changes Everything*. London: Allen Lane.

Robinson, K. and Aronica, L. (2015). *Creative Schools: Revolutionizing Education from the Ground Up*. New York: Penguin.

Rochester, C., Paine, A. E., Howlett, S., Zimmeck, M. and Ellis Paine, A. (2012). *Volunteering and Society in the 21st Century*. Basingstoke: Palgrave Macmillan.

Rose, M. (2014). *Why School? Reclaiming Education for All of Us* (Revised and expanded edn). New York: New Press.

Rowe, J. (2013). *Sorting Out Behaviour*. Carmarthen: Independent Thinking Press.

Sahlberg, P. (2012). The Most Wanted: Teachers and Teacher Education in Finland, in L. Darling-Hammond and A. Lieberman (eds), *Teacher Education Around the World: Changing Policies and Practices*. Abingdon: Routledge, pp. 1–21.

Sahlberg, P. (2015). *Finnish Lessons 2.0* (2nd edn). New York: Teachers' College Press.

Savage, J. (2010). *Cross-Curricular Teaching and Learning in Secondary Education*. Abingdon: Routledge.

Scherer, M. (ed.) (2003). *Keeping Good Teachers*. Alexandria, VA: ASCD.

Schmidt, E. and Cohen, J. (2013). *The New Digital Age: Reshaping the Future of People, Nations and Business*. London: John Murray.

Schmoker, M. (1999). *Results: The Key to Continuous School Improvement* (2nd edn). Alexandria, VA: ASCD.

Sebba, J. and Robinson, C. (2010). *Evaluation of UNICEF UK's Rights Respecting School Award*. London: UNICEF.

Seldon, A. (2015). *Beyond Happiness: The Trap of Happiness and How to Find Deeper Meaning and Joy*. London: Yellow Kite.

Seppänen, O., Fisk, W. J. and Faulkner, D. (2004). Control of Temperature for Health and Productivity in Offices. Berkeley, CA: Lawrence Berkeley National Laboratory. Available at: https://eaei.lbl.gov/sites/default/files/lbnl-55448.pdf.

Shearer, G., Vacher, K. and Hargreaves, D. H. (2007). *System Redesign 3: Curriculum Redesign*. London: Specialist Schools and Academies Trust.

Sherrington, T. (2012). Co-constructing Your Classes: Putting Pupils in the Driving Seat, *The Guardian* (8 October). Available at: https://www.theguardian.com/teacher-network/2012/oct/08/coconstructing-classes-pupils-teaching-tips.

Singer, P. (2015). *The Most Good You Can Do*. New Haven, CT: Yale University Press.

Slavin, R. (2010). Cooperative Leaning: What Makes Group-Work Work? in H. Dumont, D. Istance and F. Benavides (eds), *The Nature of Learning: Using Research to Inspire Practice*. OECD Publishing, pp. 161–178.

Smolan, R. (2013). Can Big Data Change Who You Are? [video]. Available at: https://www.youtube.com/watch?v=8CrwICToUqw.

Staricoff, M. (2013). Leadership Interview: Creating Confident Young Learners, *LDR* (autumn): 26–29. Available at: https://issuu.com/hertfordinfants/docs/ldr-october-2013.

Stratford, R. (1990). Creating a Positive School Ethos, *Educational Psychology in Practice* 5(4): 183–191.

Sutton Trust (2011). Improving the Impact of Teachers on Pupil Achievement in the UK – Interim Findings. Available at: https://www.suttontrust.com/wp-content/uploads/2011/09/2teachers-impact-report-final.pdf.

Taylor, C. (1991). *The Ethics of Authenticity*. Cambridge, MA: Harvard University Press.

Thomas, G. (2013). *How to Do Your Research Project*. London: SAGE.

Toop, J. (2013). Making the Most of Middle Leaders to Drive Change in Schools [blog], *The Guardian* (2 July). Available at: https://www.theguardian.com/teacher-network/teacher-blog/2013/jul/02/middle-leaders-driving-change-school.

Tracy, B. (2013). *Eat That Frog! Get More of the Important Things Done Today!* London: Hodder and Stoughton.

Vogue (2013). Talking with Hanya Yanagihara About Her Debut Novel, *The People in the Trees* (12 August). Available at: http://www.vogue.com/article/talking-with-hanya-yanagihara-about-her-debut-novel-the-people-in-the-trees.

Vosniadou, S. and Ortony, A. (1989). *Similarity and Analogical Reasoning: A Synthesis*. New York: Cambridge University Press.

Vygotsky, L. S. (1978). *Mind in Society: The Development of Higher Psychological Processes*. Cambridge, MA: Harvard University Press.

Wallace, M. (2001). Sharing Leadership of Schools through Teamwork: A Justifiable Risk? *Educational Management & Administration* 29(2): 153–167.

Waters, M. (2013). *Thinking Allowed on Schooling*. Carmarthen: Independent Thinking Press.

West, P., Sweeting, H. and Young, R. (2010). Transition Matters: Pupils' Experiences of the Primary–Secondary School Transition in the West of Scotland and Consequences for Well-Being and Attainment, *Research Papers in Education* 25(1): 21–50.

West-Burnham, J. and Harris, D. (2014). *Leadership Dialogues: Conversations and Activities for Leadership Teams*. Carmarthen: Crown House Publishing.

Wheatley, M. J. (2007). *Finding Our Way: Leadership for An Uncertain Time*. San Francisco, CA: Berrett-Koehler.

Wilshaw, M. (2016). Speech given at the FASNA Autumn Conference, London, 2 November. Available at: https://www.gov.uk/government/speeches/sir-michael-wilshaws-speech-at-the-fasna-autumn-conference.

Wood, P. and Smith, J. (2016). *Educational Research: Taking the Plunge*. Carmarthen: Independent Thinking Press.

Woods, P. (1990). *The Happiest Days? How Pupils Cope with School*. London: Falmer Press.

Download menu

These resources are available to download from www.crownhouse.co.uk/featured/ld2

1 Securing equity and engagement

1A The education of vulnerable and disadvantaged pupils

1A(i)

1A(ii)

1A(iii)

1B Securing inclusion

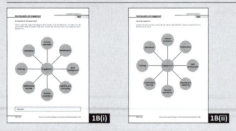

1B(i)

1B(ii)

1C Combatting exclusion

1C(i)

1C(ii)

1D Transition and induction

1D(i)

1D(ii)

1D(iii)

These resources are available to download from www.crownhouse.co.uk/featured/ld2

1E Balancing achievement and vulnerability

1E(i)

1E(ii)

2 Clarifying the purpose of education

2A What does it mean to be educated?

2A(i)

2A(ii)

2A(iii)

2B Balancing the academic and the personal

2B(i)

2B(ii)

2C Securing every child's entitlement

2C(i)

2C(ii)

2D Building consensus across the school community

2D(i)

2D(ii)

2D(iii)

2D(iv)

2E The great education debate – what is it for?

2E(i)

2E(ii)

2E(iii)

2E(iv)

3 Middle leadership – the engine room of the school

3A Subject leadership

3A(i)

3A(ii)

3A(iii)

3B Cross-curricular roles – leading strands outside the subject area

3B(i)

3B(ii)

3B(iii)

3B(iv)

These resources are available to download from www.crownhouse.co.uk/featured/ld2

3C Pastoral roles – looking after the human side

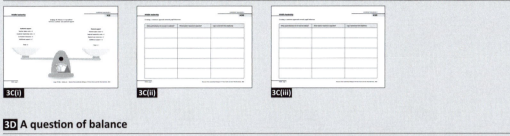

3C(i)   3C(ii)   3C(iii)

3D A question of balance

3D(i)   3D(ii)

3E Working in teams

3E(i)   3E(ii)   3E(iii)

4 Managing resources

4A Making better use of your time

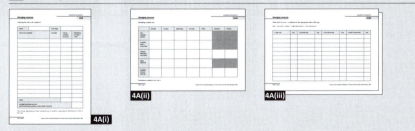

4A(i)   4A(ii)   4A(iii)

4B Meetings that work

4B(i) 4B(ii) 4B(iii)

4C After the meeting – ensuring impact

4C(i)

4D Optimising personal effectiveness

4D(i) 4D(ii)

4E High impact and low cost – cost–benefit analysis in school management

4E(i) 4E(ii)

These resources are available to download from www.crownhouse.co.uk/featured/ld2

5 Learning and technology

5A Will the genie go back in the bottle?

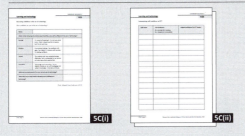

5A(i)

5A(ii)

5B The great mobile phone debate – learning tool vs. distraction

5B(i)

5B(ii)

5B(iii)

5C Educating the digital generation – digital natives

5C(i)

5C(ii)

5D Maximising the effective use of the ICT budget

5D(i)

5D(ii)

These resources are available to download from www.crownhouse.co.uk/featured/ld2

5E Using technology to enhance leadership

5E(i)

5E(ii)

6 Education beyond the school

6A What can we learn from education around the world?

6A(i)

6A(ii)

6B Citizenship for the 21st century

6B(i)

6B(ii)

6B(iii)

6C Education for sustainability

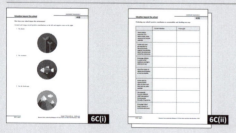

6C(i)

6C(ii)

These resources are available to download from www.crownhouse.co.uk/featured/ld2

6D Respect – demanded or given?

6D(i)   6D(ii)

6E Student leadership

6E(i)   6E(ii)

7 Alternative staffing models

7A Recruiting and retaining staff

7A(i)   7A(ii)

7B Professionalising volunteering

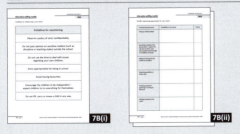

7B(i)   7B(ii)

These resources are available to download from www.crownhouse.co.uk/featured/ld2

7C Structure vs. flexibility

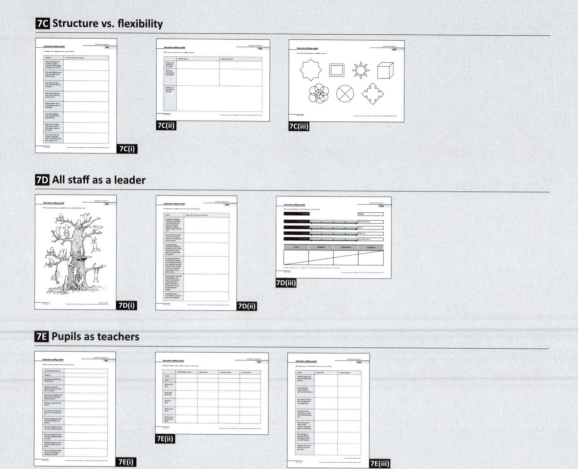

7D All staff as a leader

7E Pupils as teachers

8 Developing evidence based practice

8A Understanding educational research

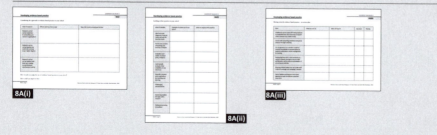

These resources are available to download from www.crownhouse.co.uk/featured/ld2

8B Research in the classroom

8B(i)

8B(ii)

8C Using research to improve practice

8C(i)

8C(ii)

8D Taking evidence from outside the education world

8D(i)

8D(ii)

8E Some research of note

8E(i)

8E(ii)